The Small Business Owner's Guide to Bankruptcy

Know You

Recover

and Start

First Edition, 2002

Published by: **Sphinx® Publishing, An Imprint of Sourcebooks, Inc.®**

<u>Naperville Office</u>
P.O. Box 4410
Naperville, Illinois 60567-4410
630-961-3900
Fax: 630-961-2168
www.sourcebooks.com
www.SphinxLegal.com

This publication is designed to provide accurate and authoritative information in regard
to the subject matter covered. It is sold with the understanding that the publisher is not
engaged in rendering legal, accounting, or other professional service. If legal advice or
other expert assistance is required, the services of a competent professional person
should be sought.

From a Declaration of Principles Jointly Adopted by a Committee of the
American Bar Association and a Committee of Publishers and Associations

Library of Congress Cataloging-in-Publication Data
Schollander, Wendell, 1943-
    The Small Business owner's guide to bankruptcy : know your legal
rights, recover from mistakes, and start over successfully / by Wendell
Schollander and Wes Shollander [i.e. Schollander].
        p. cm.
    ISBN 1-57248-219-2 (pbk.)
    1. Bankruptcy--United States--Popular works. 2. Small business--Law
and legislation--United States--Popular works. I. Schollander, Wes,
1974- II. Title.
    KF1524.6 .S36 2002
    346.7307'8--dc21
                                                    2002011478

Printed and bound in the United States of America.

VHG Paperback — 10 9 8 7 6 5 4 3 2 1

CONTENTS

Part 2: Types of Bankruptcy

Part 3: Life and Business After Filing Bankruptcy

Introduction

The small businessperson faces a host of problems and challenges in operating a business. The bookshelves are full of books with advice on how to succeed and how to make money. However, there is almost nothing that gives guidance to the eight out of ten small businesses that run into problems.

We are bankruptcy lawyers and we have long been frustrated by the mistakes people make when they face money problems. Often these mistakes are made out of a lack of knowledge about the *insolvency* process and fear of what can happen to them. This book will try to help people avoid these mistakes and endeavor to remove some of the fear by explaining how the system works.

By necessity, legal principles will have to be covered. Learning about legal issues is not easy. It is often said the law is a "seamless web." What is meant by that is when you are learning about one area you are likely to need a prior understanding of several other areas to understand the new topic. The problem, of course, is that when you are starting your study, you don't know about the other areas. If you move to learn about those other areas, they in turn will depend on a prior knowledge of even still different areas.

Thus in writing about business (and personal) bankruptcy, we will often need to cover the same areas in several different places in this book.

In our practice we see many small business people who, by the time they come to us, have taken steps that prevent them from using the bankruptcy laws to save their businesses, homes or other property. It is our goal to provide the small business owner with the information necessary to avoid these mistakes, as well as a full overview of how to navigate their business from the first hint of money problems through bankruptcy and on to financial recovery.

The organization of this work reflects the journey most people take as they face money problems and contemplate bankruptcy. Part I deals with the information gathering and review stages—a review of business organization (Section 1); why small businesspeople are more likely to face financial problems (Section 2); what bill collectors can and cannot do (Section 3); a general introduction to the types of bankruptcy (Section 4); how a businessperson's personal and business financial life intermix (Section 5); myths about debt and bankruptcy (Section 6); alternatives to bankruptcy (Section 7); what lawyers can do to help (Section 8); common mistakes people make when they have money problems (Section 9); the importance of making a financial analysis of your business' status (Section 10); how to take a personal financial inventory (Section 11); what property you may lose if you file bankruptcy (Section 12); and steps to take (and avoid) prior to bankruptcy (Section 13).

Part II deals with the bankruptcy process itself—Chapter 7, 11 and 13 bankruptcy, and the issues that can come up after you file bankruptcy (Sections 14 through 17).

Part III covers life after bankruptcy—continuing your business (Section 18), and rebuilding your credit (Section 19).

This book is designed to be read a bit at a time, rather than straight through. Depending on where you are in your financial journey, you may wish to first read about the myths of debt and bankruptcy, or what mistakes to avoid in operating your business in bad times. Since some of the same concepts apply to each area, there will need to be coverage of some of these areas in more than one place in order for each subject to make sense. We hope you will find the information and approach helpful.

PART I
BACKGROUND INFORMATION for the BUSINESSPERSON

Section 1

Types of Small Businesses and Their Operations

There are many different ways to organize a business—from sole proprietorship to sub-chapter S corporations. Over the years we have found many small business people do not know what format they are operating under. Often they think their business is a corporation because they use the word company in the business's name. Sometimes they know a lawyer or accountant "took care of legal formality" when the business was formed years ago, but they do not know what was done and have not worried about it since.

Since the "nature" of the business can have a great effect on what type of bankruptcy you or the company can file, it is worthwhile to take a minute to read over this section.

Sole Proprietorships

The most common business form in the United States is the *sole proprietorship*. All forms of business, from the corner lemonade stand to multi-million dollar companies exist as sole proprietorships. Unlike a corporation or a limited liability company (LLC), nothing needs to be filed with the government in order to bring the sole proprietorship into existence. A sole proprietorship is formed the instant a person begins operating a business without a partner or filing to change the business's status.

A sole proprietorship is the legal term for an individual operating a business without special status (such as corporate status). A sole proprietorship is merely an extension of the person who is operating the business. The business's debts are considered personal debts of the entrepreneur while the business' assets can be reached in order to satisfy the individual's personal debts. There is no legal distinction between the person and the business.

The most prevalent misconception surrounding sole proprietorships is that once the business's assets are sold off, the business' creditors cannot go after the individual's property. This is wrong. As the sole proprietorship and the entrepreneur are considered one and the same, *a debt against one is treated as a debt against the other*. The entrepreneur must incorporate or seek some other form of protection in order to protect personal property.

Partnerships

A *partnership* is formed when two or more individuals agree to operate a business without filing for special status. Partnerships are very easy to form. A partnership is usually formed once an agreement is made as to splitting profits. This agreement can be written or oral.

Once a partnership is formed, all partners are responsible for all the business' debts. A creditor can usually sue a partner for the full amount of a debt once partnership assets have been exhausted. A partnership gives no protection to its members' assets. Much like a sole proprietorship, a partnership is simply an extension of its members' estates. It is not a separate legal entity.

The great danger in a partnership is that one partner can create a debt that holds the other partner or partners accountable even if the others did not know what was done.

Corporations

Corporations are the most common form of special legal business status in the United States. Filing for corporate status shields shareholders from liability on corporate debts. The corporation is treated like a separate individual who is responsible for its own debts. Once the corporation's assets are exhausted, barring any agreements to the contrary, creditors have no further recourse.

Filing for corporate status is a relatively simple procedure. A lawyer can help you incorporate and follow your state guidelines as to how to maintain corporate status. Every state requires a corporation to meet minimal operational guidelines such as maintaining corporate procedure (i.e. electing a board of directors and holding corporate meetings) and avoiding co-mingling of corporate and individual assets. Failure to follow these corporate formalities results in the loss of the *corporate shield*. Although not overly complicated, corporate formalities are required in order to maintain the corporate shield.

The small businessperson, however, faces an even greater hurdle to preserving corporate protection than just following proper corporate procedure. Creditors know that once a corporation's assets are dissolved, barring any further agreements, they will be unable to get at the entrepreneurs personal assets. Since most small business corporations have no assets, creditors will want to have another fish on the line. This means that creditors almost always have the entrepreneur guarantee the debt. In this way, if the corporation fails and lacks the assets to pay debts, creditors can the go after the individual behind the corporation.

Be careful when signing contracts on a corporation's behalf. Most small business contracts are written by creditors who have lawyers working for them. Contracts are almost always written in a way that if the corporation fails, the entrepreneur is then liable. Unless you sign the contract "John Doe, on behalf of Corporation Inc." or something similar, more than likely you are also personally liable for the debt. It is very common for small businesspeople to insist that it is only the corporation who is liable on a debt and not them personally, then come to find out once the contract is read that they are personally liable.

Some people believe that forming an "S" corporation will provide further protection as to corporate debt or obligations as a grantor. This is not true. The "S" corporation is merely a tax device to modify income tax payments; it has no effect on corporate debts.

In theory, a corporation is a good means for a businessperson to protect his or her personal property from liability on business debts. In reality, a small businessperson will have problems maintaining corporate protection. Even if all corporate formalities are followed, creditors are loath to lend money to a small corporation without a personal guarantee.

Limited Liability Company

Thirty years ago, Limited Liability Companies (LLCs) did not exist. By 1997, every state in the country had recognized such business entities. The rapid growth in LLCs' popularity is due to the fact that LLCs offer the same protection as corporations, but there is no double taxation problem. An LLC is treated the same as a sole proprietorship or partnership for tax purposes while providing the corporate shield.

The small business entrepreneur, however, must still be careful to limit his personal liability when signing contracts. Some states may also require certain formalities for LLCs, although they tend to be less than for corporations. LLCs appear to be filling a void in American business structure, giving the security of the corporate shield without the problems of double taxation or corporate formalities. A local attorney should be able to explain your state's LLC requirements and help you to comply with them.

Section 2
The
Special Challenges
of an
Entrepreneur

This book is about small business owners and entrepreneurs who are facing money problems and considering bankruptcy. These people are anyone who owns a business where they are a key element of the business. People who have a skill they sell, such as carpenters, doctors, interpreters, or art directors; people who sell a service, such as lawn mowing services, truckers, or funeral homes; and those who sell products, such as builders, merchants or small manufacturers, are in this group.

As you read through this book you will find as many references to personal finances as to business. This is because for most small business people—the two are intertwined. Often entrepreneurs personally guarantee business loans. They often use credit cards and personal loans to tide them over when the business is not producing sufficient income to live on. Many times they personally own the vehicles and equipment the business is using, or their personal car is owned by the corporation. For this reason, any time a small business owner is forced to consider business bankruptcy, his or her personal financial status must be examined along with the business's finances.

Double-sided Pressure

The small businessperson is often under pressure on two fronts. First, the business operation can come across a host of possible problems, including the normal problems that can affect anyone—sickness, injury and family problems. When times turn bad the business encounters the second front—collection calls and lawsuits by business creditors as well as personal creditors. To this must be added fears about the future of a businessperson's livelihood. The pressure can be overwhelming, and the worst part is that the businessperson is often facing this pressure alone.

Reasons for Money Problems

After interviewing thousands of business people who are experiencing debt problems or money stress, it is discovered that they almost inevitably experience those money problems because:

- customers run into their own cash flow problems or just will not pay;
- a business recession or other change in the general economic climate causes a drop in orders;
- new competitors are keeping prices down; or,
- costs have increased more than prices can be raised.

None of these problems have been caused by the businessperson. They are the product of a "dog-eat-dog" business system.

To these business problems must be added the problems the person can have in his or her personal life. He or she can have a relationship break-up and end up with bills for two, or experience medical debt often combined with an income loss because of the sickness or injury, for example.

Because the small businessperson often finds his personal and business life intertwined, debts for one often serve as funds for the other. For this reason, trends in personal finance are very important for the businessperson.

Another problem is that incomes for the average person (including the business owner) are not rising as fast as the cost of living. Over the last fifteen or twenty years the average person has lost ground financially. This has two effects. First, business people often operate close to the edge with little room for error. Second, they create an increase in debt as people try to maintain their business and their standard of living. This larger debt overhang in turn makes them more vulnerable to medical emergencies, loss of income, personal tragedies, divorce, or separation.

Debt More Specifically

Debt is more deadly now than it was in the past. Interest rates are much higher than they were fifty years ago. In the late 1970's, credit card issuers and other creditors were able to increase the interest rates of their cards and loans. Court interpretations of banking laws allowed financial institutions to place credit card operations in states that permitted high interest rate charges and to sell the cards into states that tried to enforce the traditionally lower interest rates. In time, other states increased their maximum interest charges in an effort to retain or attract credit card operations and keep their lenders competitive.

The reason high interest rates were traditionally not allowed prior to the late 1970's was that everyone knew that once a person or business got behind on an 18 percent interest rate, or even on a 12 percent interest rate, it was nearly impossible to get caught up. In fact, it is very difficult to ever pay off a debt at a 12 to 18 percent interest rate because most of the payments are going to interest. If you make the minimum payments on a debt with an 18 percent interest rate, it will take you over fourteen years to pay off the debt.

Downward Spiral

One of the problems with having a financial crisis is there is really very little one can do about it over the short run. If business slows down or a person gets sick and cannot work for a month or two, there is little adjustment that can be made in their fixed overhead cost of living. Things such as rent, equipment leases, vehicle payments, and mortgage are fixed. The only places one can cut back are on food, entertainment, and perhaps clothing. Without an emergency reserve, if there is not enough flexibility in those three areas, a person must then cut back on what is sent to creditors and suppliers each month. This leads to a vicious spiral downward.

Creditors will charge late fees and the interest rate will keep compounding as they charge interest on the interest that accumulated from the months before. Quite often before the person knows it, they are deeply in debt. What then typically follows is a desperate struggle to keep the creditors at bay. This is typically referred to as "robbing Peter to pay Paul" (paying one creditor one month and then skipping a month while another creditor is paid, dodging phone calls, and getting cash advances to pay creditors). All of this pulls the person and the business deeper and deeper into debt.

Generally, people want very badly to pay their debts. That is the way they were brought up and they believe it is the right thing to do. They also do not like the feeling of paying their bills in an untimely, inefficient way. Not being able to pay the obligations creates feelings of guilt and failure and the collection calls and letters add stress. This creates a typical pattern of psychological and physical stress that will be covered next.

Effects of Financial Pressure

People we have interviewed reported a typical pattern of problems and symptoms when under financial pressure:

- insomnia;
- sickness and accidents;
- fights with a spouse or partner;
- problems at work;
- headaches;
- avoidance;
- depression; and,
- grief.

Perhaps you recognize yourself in this picture. People often do not realize how much pressure they are under because of debt stress until it is released. The pressure built up slowly and they adjusted to it each time as it built up. But it is definitely there.

They often say things such as, "I'm forty years old, and I've worked hard all my life. I never thought I would be in a position where I was not able to pay my debts," or, "I live in a nice neighborhood and all my neighbors think I have an ideal life. I never thought this would be happening to me. No one knows what I'm going through. I don't know what I'm going to do."

Veterans of Vietnam and the Persian Gulf often say it was worse than being in combat. "I told myself that if I lived through this war nothing would ever bother me again—but this is worse than the fear of being killed." In fact, some in a debt crisis want to die. Many debtors report they have thoughts about suicide.

One very common concern are feelings of guilt and shame. They do not want others to know. People do not want their parents or children to find out they have money problems, and they certainly do not want their neighbors and co-workers to find out. The effect of this is to isolate the individual and to prevent the stress from being released.

They do not realize how many other people have the same problem. There are a million cases each year moving through the bankruptcy court, and many more cases being dealt with through Consumer Credit Counseling and other businesses handling debt problems. It is the rare business that at some point does not have money problems. But, debt problems are largely a hidden epidemic. Since everyone is hiding their problem, everyone thinks they are the only one to have such problems. These debt problems cut right across all financial strata. We have had many people come to us who had been making $100,000 or more a year and had almost had their homes foreclosed.

One answer to avoiding financial problems that arise from a cut in income or medical expenses is to have an emergency fund set aside. Experts recommend a reserve of ready money equal to six to ten months of income. While this is good advice, in practice almost no one can follow it. High tax rates make it hard to make enough money to merely keep the business going and to raise a family.

The entrepreneur's natural instinct is to invest profits back into the business to make it grow. Trying to save a half year's income from after-tax money is very hard, financially and psychologically. And if you should do it, what do you do with it? Most people will invest these funds in stocks. When a recession hits they often get a double blow—they lose their job and the value of their nest egg drops.

Section 3

The Dangers of Past Due Debts, Bankruptcy and the Collection Process

Because they are under pressure from two sides, small businesspeople must worry about the action of both business creditors and personal creditors. People collecting for creditors will often threaten or seem to threaten all types of dire actions—some of which they cannot legally do. It is good to have an idea of what can, and more importantly, cannot be done.

Business Creditors

A creditor who has a claim against a business alone has a limited number of options. They can and will, as a first measure, cut off future credit and sales. Creditors who have interest in equipment and inventory may try to have the property turned over to them voluntarily, often with a threat of a lawsuit if this is not done. In certain cases, equipment may be seized. It is fairly unusual for a large business creditor to call you at home or contact family or co-workers, but it does happen in some cases. Banks may *accelerate* (ask for full payment) loans and *freeze* (prohibit any withdrawal) money held in your account to cover debts owed to them.

Personal Creditors

In the great majority of cases where there is a money problem with a small business, it transforms itself into an issue of personal debt and the entrepreneur must deal with personal creditors. There are two reasons for this. First, most banks or businesses will not loan money, lease equipment, or rent space to a business without *personal guarantees* (guarantee in a person's name rather than the business). Second, the businessperson often uses his personal credit to obtain funds for the business, or to operate the business. We have all heard of the producer who made a movie using cash advances from credit cards, or the businessperson who lived on credit cards while waiting for the business to get off the ground, or during a slow period for the business.

It is normally the *personal debts* the small business has accrued that drives the owner to see a lawyer, as these tend to be the ones putting a great deal of the stress on the individual. Quite often business people turn to credit cards or personal loans from finance companies to bridge short falls in business income. In addition, they give their homes and personal vehicles as collateral for loans to use in the business.

Steps the Creditor Cannot Take

Owing money you cannot pay is stressful partly because you feel guilty, and perhaps like a failure. The other source of stress is bill collectors and their tactics. When you start receiving phone calls from collections people they are often quite aggressive if not abusive. We have been told many times that creditors threaten to have the debtor arrested and put in jail, or to have his or her salary or taxes garnished. Creditors often tell people that it is fraud to not pay back money borrowed.

Jail

One cannot be arrested and put in jail for a civil debt owed to a credit card company or a bank. Normally the only time you are put in jail is when you break a law or fail to obey an order of the court in a family matter. Owing money to a person is not a crime and is not something for which you can be jailed. The United States has done away with debtors' prison. Nowhere can a creditor seize your pay check or property without a law suit and the chance for you to have a trial.

Seizing Property

Creditors will sometimes say things such as "We are going to take all your property," or if they are particularly sadistic, say, "We are going to take your kids' furniture and pets." People have visions of their things being taken from their home and piled up on their front yard for everyone to see. This is almost certain to never happen, so try not to let this threat bother you. A creditor cannot just get a policeman and start hauling furniture out of your house. Even if they want the furniture, they will have to get a court order before they can invade your home or office. This means they will have to go to the expense of a lawsuit.

Tax Refunds

A private company cannot have the government seize your tax refunds. If you owe taxes or owe money on a government guaranteed student loan, then you can have your tax refund seized, but a private company cannot do this. If someone who is not of a government entity or collecting for a government entity threatens to do one of these, take it with a very large grain of salt.

Wage Garnishment

It is quite common for creditors to threaten to have your wages *garnished* (money removed directly from your paycheck to send to the creditors). This is a powerful collection tool if you are earning a wage, but of limited use against a self employed individual. In addition, not every state allows wage garnishment.

Harassment

Given the limited range of what a collector can do without a lawsuit, they often start by pestering or harassing you to distraction. We have had reports of people getting calls from the same creditor two and three times a day. Calls start at seven o'clock in the morning and go to eleven o'clock at night. Collectors often call debtors at work after being asked not to, and many times the receptionist, the boss or employees are told about the person's debt problems. Family members are often called and told about the person's debt problems. We have even had cases where the collection people talked to neighbors and told them the person was not paying their bills.

Books on debt management often advise readers who are having extensive financial problems to contact their creditors, explain the situation to them and try to work out a reduced payment schedule. In our experience this almost never works. It may be possible to work out something with one creditor, but if there are several, there are almost always some who will not work with you and insist on full payment. Some will insult you as you pour out your heart to them. Unless all creditors agree to a reduced payment, it's unlikely that setting up a system of reduced payments will work.

The other problem with this advice is that you often talk to a different person every time you call the creditor or the collection agency. You can make an agreement with one person at the agency, and then a few days later get an abusive collection call from someone else at the same company. When you try to explain to the new person that you have worked out a reduced payment plan, they often will deny any knowledge of it and demand full payment at once. Often they will say, "I have never heard of that person," or, "There is no such arrangement noted in the computer." It is emotionally exhausting trying to explain the same thing over and over again every few days while being abused.

We have heard this sequence of events told to us so often that we are convinced the collectors are using one or two techniques. One is "good cop - bad cop," where one collector will be nice and understanding and the next will be hateful and try to break you down. The other is the "wolf pack method". (When wolves hunt a deer one doesn't run up and kill the deer. Rather they will take turns running up to the animal and biting a bit of flesh away. No one bite kills the deer. The deer bleeds to death or just gives up in exhaustion.)

Laws Against Harassment

People who are subject to harassing collection actions often ask whether there are laws against what their creditors are doing—calling three to four times a day, plus calling co-workers, the family, the neighbors. There are federal laws, and many states have laws against unfair collections tactics.

But, these laws are of little real practical help. You are having money problems; that's why they're calling you. Do you have the money to hire a lawyer to bring a state court lawsuit, much less a federal lawsuit, against them? Do you even know who to sue? Most of the time they're just a voice on the phone. They could be down the street or across the country. What address do you send the law suit papers to? Do you really know the name of the caller or their company? Many of them use fake names.

If you overcome all of these problems and get to court, then it's your and your friends' word against theirs. We have talked to some of the collectors whose clients said they were calling family and neighbors. They always say with great sincerity, "We would never take an illegal action." They know a lot more about how the collection laws work than you do, and odds are that if the question came to trial they could talk their way out of a judgment against them.

Consumer protection agencies

What about the consumer protection agencies? Government agencies and consumer protection lawyers are set up to do *class action* (groups of people with similar issues) lawsuits rather than help individuals.

Basically, you are on your own and as a practical matter the creditors can do just about anything they want. There are only two avenues to get help. One is Consumer Credit Counseling and the other is a Private Debt Manager who, if you can pay enough, may be able to set up a payment program that will satisfy all your creditors. These options will be covered in detail in Section 7.

Steps the Creditor Can Take

One of the first things business suppliers do is stop supplying products, or put you on C.O.D. (cash on delivery) when you lag on payments. Both of these badly hamper those businesses that depend on credit from suppliers. But, there are many businesses not affected by this type of pressure, such as freight haulers, doctors, lawyers, carpenters, service providers, etc. Their normal mode of operation is to pay for supplies at the time they receive them. Reasonable phone calls from lenders or suppliers who need their money to stay in business are allowed.

Lawsuit

When creditors give up on calling you the next step is a lawsuit. Suing you is not an abusive collection method. You owe the money and the creditor has the right to go to court to try to collect it.

People are often thrown into a panic when they first hear about a lawsuit. Some creditors will describe a lawsuit in such a way as to make people think they will be put in jail. They use words such as, "I'll send the sheriff out with papers."

As noted above, you cannot be put in jail for a civil debt. The normal way to serve lawsuit papers is to have a sheriff or other process server deliver them. Sometimes they are simply mailed to you. But service by sheriff is a favored threat since it upsets people, and people fear the vision of having a law officer come to where they work or live and serve papers on them in front of co-workers or neighbors.

When the papers are served they often say you have so many days to answer (often thirty days) or that you must answer within so many days. You will not get in trouble if you do not give the court an answer or go to court. It is only criminal court where you can be arrested for not appearing in court. Debt collection lawsuits are civil suits. In fact, there is not much point in going to court if you are being sued for a debt and owe the money. The court cannot excuse you because you have had bad breaks, so going and telling your story does not help at all.

Judgment against you

A judgment against you may have very little effect, or it can be a disaster. The collection process after a lawsuit or foreclosure hearing is the danger point for any debtor.

Creditors are allowed to take steps to collect a judgment and now they have a court order on their side. In cases of secured property, the court will direct that the property be turned over to the creditor, if the creditor has not been able to pick it up on its own.

Seizing property and the exemption form

Another step is to have a sheriff take the debtors' other property to collect the judgment. Normally this involves first sending notice to the debtors that they have the right to protect certain assets if they are listed on a form turned into the court within a limited number of days. Since the form is often a bit complicated, and since ignoring the creditor has worked in the past, some people do not fill out the form. This is a serious mistake. If the form is not filled out the creditor can seize any property the debtor owns, often including their home. A favorite target when the debtor does not fill out this exemption form is the debtor's car. This puts maximum pressure on the debtor as he or she needs the car to get to work and there is a ready market for used cars.

The form normally has different types of property that can be protected. Depending on the state, this protected property area may be sufficiently generous that the creditor cannot seize any property. Should this be the case the debtor is said to be judgment proof.

If your property in a given category is worth more than can be protected, which is often the case for business owners, the creditor can send a sheriff out to pick it up and sell it. At these sales the property is often sold for far less than it is worth. This amount is subtracted from the amount owed and the debtor is still responsible for the remaining debt.

Judgment Lien

There is another way a judgment can harm a debtor. The judgment becomes a *judgment lien* against land and homes, where when the property is sold, the money must be paid. Land other than a person's home can often be taken at once. (It is harder to make a general statement about a person's home. It may be protected or not depending on the state one lives in.) Even if a home is not taken at once, it has a judgment lien against it, which means when the home is sold the judgment must be paid.

For example:

Suppose Sue owns a home worth $100,000 in a state where she can protect $10,000 of home equity. There is a judgment lien against the home for $3,000. She owes $95,000 so she only has $5,000 worth of equity ($100,000 − $95,000 = $5,000). Her home is protected.

However, if she should sell the home the $95,000 mortgage and the judgment lien must be paid from the money she receives for the sale of her home.

Because of this fact, creditors often times do not bother with trying to take personal assets, but merely wait for the debtor to sell his or her home. They know that almost all buyers will require any judgment lien to be paid off as part of the purchase of the land or home.

Foreclosure

Another legal process that may come into play is *foreclosure* (forced sale of a home by a lender). It is common for business people to let home payments slide while they devote all their time and money to keeping the business going. Foreclosure is threatened more often than it is done because creditors know it will upset the home owner. The creditor does not really want your home if there is a good chance they can get the money owed them in a reasonable, timely way. Creditors, however, will often be demanding about house payments because they know they have such a powerful weapon to use against you.

The foreclosure process works as follows:

- First you are served a notice of a legal hearing. This gives you the chance to offer any legal defense you may have. Having illness or other problems is not a legal defense. You do not have to attend this hearing, and your time would be better spent talking to a lawyer about bankruptcy since some bankruptcy procedures can stop a foreclosure.

- Once the foreclosure hearing has been held the property is advertised for a foreclosure sale. Since these advertisements are designed to inform as many people as possible about the availability of the property, they can be quite embarrassing.

- On the sale day the property is auctioned off to the highest bidder. This is often done in an obscure part of the local courthouse. After the sale is done there is often a limited amount of time for an upset bid. At the end of the process your home is no longer yours and you must move out.

NOTE Bankruptcy is a powerful tool to stop a foreclosure. You may not qualify, but rather than lose your home, you should investigate the possibility.

Exceptions to the Need for Court Proceedings

There are two notable exceptions to starting a lawsuit first. One is the *right of off-set*. If you owe money to a bank or credit union and have money on deposit there, the bank or credit union can take enough of your money to pay off all or part of the debt. This is called the right of off-set. Be careful to remove any money from any financial institution that you owe money to. If you are in a financial crisis your budget is tight, and it will be even tighter if the bank seizes what little money you have on hand to pay the rent or buy food.

The other exception is the right of repossession. A creditor who loaned you the money to buy your equipment, car, or truck can take the equipment or vehicle back if they have a *security interest* in the vehicle. (*Leasors* (those who lend things on lease) can take back leased equipment since it belongs to them. No one else can take it without a court order or permission.) If creditors have a security interest they can take the property and sell it to recover the money you owe them. They cannot use force or violence to take the property and often must stop if you act like you will fight them for it. This is why repossessions are often done at night or while a businessperson is away. They are not allowed to trespass on private property to do their work, but since they often act when no one is around some violate this rule. Once they have the vehicle it is your word against theirs as to where the car was parked.

Once they have the property they will give you a little time to pay off the loan, and if you do not (often they want the entire loan amount) the property is sold at auction. The auction sale price is almost always far less than what you owe on the property. You are responsible for the difference between what you promised to pay and what they received for it at the auction. This difference is called the *deficiency*. The debt is not extinguished merely because they have the property back—you still owe the money you promised to pay them, less the bit the creditor received at auction. This is why a voluntary surrender does not help you. You will still be responsible for the deficiency after the property is sold. Often the fact that you voluntarily gave it back does not even help you on your credit report. A voluntary surrender is often shown as a *repossession*.

Section 4

Overview of Bankruptcy and How it Works

People speak generally of bankruptcy without realizing that there are several different types of bankruptcy that operate quite differently. An individual or a corporation can apply for a Chapter 7 or 11 bankruptcy. Only an individual can apply for a Chapter 13 bankruptcy. In bankruptcy an individual, but not a corporation, can exempt (protect) certain property necessary to live—normally shelter, personal property and transportation. These, however, are often quite limited protections. (see Appendix B.)

Chapter 7

Chapter 7 is the type most people have in mind when they speak of bankruptcy. It can be filed by either an individual or a corporation. It will wipe out many debts in their entirety. Thus, if your business owed $40,000 on credit cards, medical bills and suppliers obligations, it would completely eliminate them. Some debts such as certain taxes, secured loans, student loans, and alimony are not wiped out. You must continue to make payments on your home if you wish to keep it, and you will need to pay money for back taxes or make arrangements with the taxing authority.

The trade-off for the clean, relatively debt-free, fresh start of a Chapter 7 is that your personal or business assets can be taken and sold by the court system. The money from the sale would be distributed to your creditors. However, there are exceptions to this rule that in many cases swallow up the general rule of losing your property.

Each person who files a Chapter 7 bankruptcy will, depending on what state he or she lives in, have a list of the property and dollar limit he or she can retain. In most cases this will mean that the debtor keeps the home, furniture, cars, and personal property. Of course, since these items are often *security* (collateral) for debt, they must be paid for in monthly payments as originally contracted, as secured goods. On the other hand, business assets are not really protected, and filers often end up losing their equipment and supplies. As will be covered later, this is true whether or not the business is incorporated.

Chapter 11

When one reads in the newspaper about a business filing bankruptcy, it is usually a Chapter 11. Thus, most small businesspeople and indeed many non-business people think of Chapter 11 when they think of bankruptcy. These bankruptcies are news items because they affect a great number of people, many jobs are at stake, and many other businesses have business relationships with the entity filing the Chapter 11. Through this news coverage people know that Chapter 11 is the bankruptcy provision for businesses, although typically they know little about the process.

This popular perception is not correct. An individual, as well as a business, can file a Chapter 11 bankruptcy. However, for reasons we shall examine below, a Chapter 11 is often not suitable for a small business. There are several problems with Chapter 11 bankruptcies from the point of view of a small businessperson. First, the same basic steps and reports must be followed if you are a huge national company or a small one-store operation. This makes Chapter 11 bankruptcies quite expensive.

The second problem is that the underlying purpose of a Chapter 11 is to allow the company time to renegotiate fixed contracts and dispose of unprofitable assets in an orderly way. If you are a one-person operation selling your skills—a painter or a lawyer, for example—

there are unlikely to be fixed contracts to renegotiate or unprofitable assets to give away. If you have only a one-store location that is not generating sufficient sales to cover your expenses or earn a profit, the problem is your core business, not the contracts or extra locations. A Chapter 11 allows you an orderly way to cut overhead.

In a Chapter 11 the business manager or owner files for bankruptcy to stop collection efforts by creditors. The business continues to operate under the direction of the court. Often the management of the business stays in place and runs the business while the details are worked out.

NOTE The main trouble with a Chapter 11 for a small business is that the rules and procedures are designed for a large business, like a national airline or manufacture.

When a Chapter 11 bankruptcy is filed, the lawyers of the creditors often come post haste into court to try to protect themselves, and you must often pay your lawyer large sums of money to fight. Since the court has taken control of the business assets, it requires the business to file special periodic reports explaining the ongoing financial health of the business and what the managers are doing. This often requires special accountants and always takes a great deal of the manager's time. Normally the bankruptcy lawyer will require a very large payment up front before he or she undertakes to file a Chapter 11 because of the system's complexity, the stringent drafting requirements, and the many trips to court.

The whole process is designed to establish a plan of reorganization. The plan will detail how each group or class of creditors is to be treated and who will receive what. Each class (as a group) then votes on the plan. The plan is approved only if it meets a number of complex rules. These rules are beyond the scope of this short overview. The plan must receive the approval of a certain number of the classes. This is very different from a Chapter 7 where approval of the creditors either individually or by groups in a vote is not required.

Of course, no lawyer would just draw up a plan and present it for a vote without checking on how key members of the different groups are likely to vote. There is often a great deal of talking among the lawyers for the filer and the different creditors, all of which cost money.

The need for a team of accountants, lawyers, and managers to deal with the bankruptcy issues does not matter all that much to a Fortune Five Hundred Company but will swamp a small business. For this reason small businesses seldom file a Chapter 11, and those who do, often end up converting to a Chapter 7.

Chapter 12

Congress has enacted the Chapter 12 bankruptcy provisions to meet the special problems faced by farmers. A farmer has expenses each month, but income from the sale of animals, fruits, and grains typically come once or twice a year. While the farmer is a small businessperson, most small businessmen are not farmers. Therefore, a Chapter 12 bankruptcy will not apply to the overwhelming number of business owners.

Chapter 13

The Chapter 13 bankruptcy is often called a *wage-earner plan* or a *debt consolidation plan*. It was originally set up for employees who have a steady regular income and who could, if given time, pay at least a portion of their debts. Gradually the protection of a Chapter 13 was expanded to include people who did not have a steady income, for example salespeople and waitstaff.

In a Chapter 13 bankruptcy, the debtor discloses his or her income and sets up a plan for paying creditors over a three to five-year period. The debtor is not as likely to have assets at risk of being taken as under a Chapter 7 bankruptcy because money is being paid to the creditors. The steady monthly payments (often by wage deduction) that the debtor makes to the Chapter 13 trustee is distributed to the different creditors in accordance with a unitary plan of repayment that the debtor filed with the bankruptcy court. In these ways it is much like a Chapter 11 bankruptcy.

Comparing the types of Bankruptcies

The main difference between Chapter 11 and Chapter 13 cases is one of scale and oversight. Because Chapter 13s are dealing with smaller dollar amounts and there are so many Chapter 13s filed, there is less oversight by the court and often less involvement of creditors.

In the regulatory system set up by Congress, there are provisions for continuing to operate large businesses (Chapter 11), farms (Chapter 12) and for individual workers (Chapter 13), but there is nothing designed for the special problems of small business owners and operators. This means that a small entrepreneur who wants to keep on running a business must try to fit into the provisions of a Chapter 13 or a Chapter 11, or file a Chapter 7 and start over. Which one the small business owner uses will depend on their goals. If they are willing to give up personal and business assets, they would choose a Chapter 7. If they wish to keep running the business, their only options are Chapter 11 or 13. As noted above a Chapter 11 is not a realistic option for most small businesspeople. This leaves a Chapter 13—the wage earner's plan.

In a Chapter 13, the owner works out how much profit the business makes after paying business expenses (rent, gas, supplies, etc.). This profit is then applied to purely personal living expenses and to pay money into the court (a Chapter 13 trustee) for payment to creditors.

Section 5
The Interplay of Business and Personal Debt

Businesses need credit. Supplies have to be ordered and money is needed to tide the business over until customers pay for the goods or services provided, but few creditors will lend to a small business without a *personal guarantee* from the business owner. Thus the business' s and the proprietor's finances rapidly become intertwined. This connection comes at several stages.

When the business is just beginning, tools, equipment and supplies have to be purchased in order to be able to have a product to sell. The ultimate source of the funds for these expenditures is the money and credit of the proprietor. He or she, in turn, has only a few sources of funds. A few will have personal savings or relatives and friends who are willing to invest enough to buy these goods outright. Most will need to borrow from a bank or other financial institution. As noted earlier, banks will not loan without some guarantee. A few people will have sufficient credit standing to obtain unsecured loans (getting money without collateral), but most will need to pledge an asset such as the business equipment, their home, their car, etc. Landlords will typically require that individuals sign leases rather than having the lease only in a company name.

Then there is the *start-up phase*. Most businesses do the work, and get paid when the work is completely or partially completed. Unless the business is a part time or second job type of operation, this means taking on more debt to tide you over until the funds start coming in. This phase can last a long time. It is not uncommon for a business to be unprofitable for as much as a year or two. During this period, proprietors often turn to credit cards, or if they are lucky, draw on a line of credit secured by their start-up loan.

The next period when personal and business finances become intertwined is while the business is operating successfully. Proprietors will often begin using a company car for their transportation. They may buy items like cars, tools, trucks and computers themselves and take them to the business operation for use by the business. Many times it is very hard to reconstruct what belongs to whom. The proprietor will forget he bought the car he is driving in the company name or that the company work truck was bought by him personally.

At least with vehicles there are titles to look at. With computers, office equipment and work tools it is much harder. For example, proprietors often go to the computer store and pay for the computer personally and take it to the office, or they may take a computer bought with company funds home for personal use.

The next stage is when the business begins to hit rough spots. It is the end of the week or the month and there is not enough money for payroll. The proprietor may have only one source of money, his personal bank account. Even if the business has enough money for the payroll, the proprietor's family must be fed and his or her personal bills paid. If the business is not generating enough to cover this, the proprietor will use personal funds to tide him or her over. If he or she is lucky he or she can do so by drawing money out of savings. If not, he or she must use a credit card or a line of credit. Typically the proprietor has difficulty in obtaining a loan to cover expenses during these business slow downs, either because a bank will not loan to someone who does not have good cash flow or because it will take too long for the loan to go through.

The last stage is when slow times become chronic. There is too little money coming in for too many periods of time. Of course, expenses are cut, but one can cut only so deep without killing the business. Somewhere along the way proprietors often make a mistake that will be discussed further in Section 9, especially if it has been a long time since the proprietor paid himself or herself or took a draw and personal debit is exhausted. All too often the proprietor does not forward sales tax to the government, or does not send the money withheld from employee payrolls. This creates a personal liability for the proprietor and officers of the company. This creates another debt—this time to the government. Or sometimes owners will not file their income taxes, figuring they can cross the bridge of tax liability when they get the business back on its feet.

In addition to business connected debts, the proprietor has all the situations that create debt in the general public. Proprietors have marriages break up, they or their family gets sick and accrue doctor and hospital bills. Their cars break down, furnaces give out and roofs leak. All of these put a strain on the owner's personal finances. And it is the owner's personal financial health that is often the underpinning for the business cash reserve. If something like this happens in the proprietor's personal life, the business may be starved for money or attention. An owner who is home sick or injured cannot run the business.

For these reasons, a small business owner is much more likely to have money problems than a person working for a wage or salary.

Section 6
Myths about Debt and Bankruptcy

When people consider bankruptcy for themselves or their business, they experience all sorts of vague fears based on snippets of information they have heard over the years, advice from well-meaning friends and family and the rising of their own fears and concerns.

The most common concerns (each discussed separately in this chapter) are:

- it will ruin my credit;
- notice of my bankruptcy will be put in the newspaper, or become public;
- it will ruin my spouse's credit;
- I will lose my home and cars;
- I will lose all my other property;
- they will sell my property at auction in front of my home;
- if I file bankruptcy my spouse will have to file also;
- my spouse and I will lose our jobs;
- I will lose my license;
- I cannot get student loans;
- I cannot have a bank account;
- I will be put in jail if I do not pay my bills;
- the debts will just go away in time; and,
- I can never have credit again.

It Will Ruin My Credit

It is not uncommon for people considering bankruptcy to have very good credit. Over the years they have been careful to pay their bills on time and as a consequence have been able to borrow large sums of money. Then something happens—loss of income, illness, injury or divorce. Because of one or more of these they begin to have trouble paying their bills on time. Often people will hold off financial problems by going into savings and selling assets. But, the day comes when they do not have the funds to make their monthly payments for debts.

Normally people hold on, hoping for a turn of tides as the collection calls from creditors increase in volume and harshness. In most cases it is only then that people begin to think about bankruptcy and see a lawyer.

Reading about bankruptcy or seeing a lawyer is a symptom of financial problems. If one concludes bankruptcy is the only way to address one's financial problems, it is not the bankruptcy that is going to ruin one's credit. The person's credit status is already in trouble. To put it in medical terms, a fever is not what makes you sick—the fever is a symptom of an underlying bodily illness or injury. Bankruptcy is the financial fever and is the symptom of the underlying financial problem. A bankruptcy notation on your credit report is a strong negative, but so are car repossessions, home foreclosures, many slow pays and a high debt load. The key is to see if you are any worse off with a bankruptcy.

Notice of My Bankruptcy Will be Put into the Newspaper or Become Public

People are embarrassed when they face financial problems. It is often viewed as a prime capitalist sin. They want their financial affairs to be strictly private. For this reason, they often worry that the fact they filed bankruptcy will be put in the paper. They have vague memories of reading about bankruptcy filings, but they were busy and did not really read the story.

Rest assured, there is almost no chance your personal bankruptcy will end up in the newspaper. When the newspaper stories about bankruptcy are re-examined, they always turn out to be about large companies with many employees and suppliers—the type of thing that will interest a broad readership. Your personal bankruptcy filing is of limited interest to readers and not worth the limited space a newspaper has in its daily or weekly edition. In theory the bankruptcy of a well-known small business could cause a press story. However, in practice this almost never happens.

However, one cannot entirely rule out the possibility that the news would be put in the paper. Some small local papers are very hard up for items to put in the paper and, in theory, could choose to print the filing of your bankruptcy. Bankruptcy filings are public records and someone can go to the bankruptcy courthouse and look up bankruptcy filings. However, even then the odds are very low. Bankruptcy courts cover a very large population base and normally many counties are under the jurisdiction of the court. This means a very large number of filings will have to be searched to locate the ones that would have any possible significance to the few readers of the small local paper. This is not a good use of the newspaper's limited resources.

Another factor protecting your privacy is that most newspapers view this type of personal problem as beyond the scope of what a newspaper should cover. They are not gossip sheets or purveyors of personal problems.

A business owner faces only slightly less risk of having his or her personal financial affairs made public. If it turns out you file for personal bankruptcy, the above discussion will likely apply to you also. Of course when your business is no longer open or supplying services, customers will know something is wrong. But, they are unlikely to know exactly what. Businesses close all the time—sometimes because finances overwhelmed them and sometimes because it is no longer worth the owner's effort to keep the business going. It is just not making sufficient money to satisfy the owner. The customer will never know which is which and thus will never know the full story.

In some bankruptcy cases the business has assets that the trustee will try to sell either at a liquidation sale or by auction. However, it takes a fairly large business with a high number of assets to make either one of those procedures worthwhile to the trustee. It takes time and money to hold a sale or an auction of goods. Most small businesses do not have enough property to make a special sale of the business, inventory, or assets cost-effective for the trustee. He or she is much more likely to sell the items by private sale through a private network. He or she will sell to buyers he or she has developed relationships with or sell the items as part of a larger auction of many items from many different sources.

We must reiterate, however, that bankruptcies are *matters of public record*. That means there will be a file at the bankruptcy courthouse that can be examined by any member of the public. The same is true of the records of most lawsuits at the county courthouse. But, accessing these records is not easy. There are too many for someone to just thumb through, and they must have your specific name to pull your file. This makes it very unlikely a friend or neighbor will just stumble on your file. And of course, there is the time and effort involved in physically going to the courthouse—something almost no one is willing to take the trouble to do.

There is a movement underway to allow access to court and bankruptcy records through the Internet. This removes one barrier of finding out about bankruptcy—the physical effort. The records can be reached from a home or business. However, this search is not very easy. The layout of the web page is government-designed and is not made for ease of use. It takes a great deal more effort to navigate the website than most people are willing to undertake. It is not designed for browsing. You must have a specific name or case number to pull up a file. This makes it unlikely that anyone will, by accident, stumble upon the fact that you filed bankruptcy.

Some businesses systematically go through bankruptcy filings for their own commercial purposes. The credit union does this. Some banks or groups of banks collect this information. Credit card companies, lenders and mortgage brokers also systematically search the bankruptcy records. Their purpose is to make offers to you for credit cards or new loans. Thus, to sum up, as far as publishing the filing of your bankruptcy, the most likely result will be to put you on additional mailing lists for credit cards and loans.

It Will Ruin My Spouse's Credit

People are naturally worried about their spouse or future spouses. They say things like, "My wife (or husband) had nothing to do with the business—I don't want their credit hurt," or, "I'm about to get married, will the bankruptcy affect my spouse's credit?" (A variation of the last question is, "Will my spouse be responsible for my debts?")

Barring a mistake on the part of the credit bureau or a creditor, spouses are not affected if one member of a marriage files or has filed bankruptcy. Each person has a separate file at the credit bureau and is tracked by their social security number. Thus, assuming the spouse is not a co-debtor, wiping out a debt in bankruptcy by one member of a marriage should not affect the credit of the spouse.

Some creditors will try to tell a spouse you must pay this debt, because you are married to the debtor. This is only a collection tactic that takes advantage of people's lack of knowledge about the law.

Occasionally a debt or bankruptcy will show up reported on a spouse's credit file. This is almost always removed when the spouse objects to the entry because there is no legal basis for such a claim. Furthermore, the creditor and credit bureau can get sued if it is not corrected.

Of course, if the spouse (or other family member) is a co-debtor, then the debt and the bankruptcy will affect the spouse (or other family member). Each co-debtor is responsible for all of the debt and if one does not pay, the creditors can take collection efforts against the other co-debtor.

I Will Lose My Home and Cars

This is a realistic possibility depending on what state you live in. Most states allow people who file bankruptcy to retain a home and a car up to a certain value. The value of homes will range from unlimited value in Texas and Florida to nothing in Delaware and Pennsylvania. Most states range from $5,000 to $30,000. This is free equity in the home, so the amount of mortgage(s) must be deducted from the market value to obtain the free value of the house. Clearly if you own your home free of all debt you will (in most states) lose it in bankruptcy. But, most businesspeople, between starting their business and trying to keep it afloat, have borrowed against their homes before they consider bankruptcy, so their free equity in the home is limited.

 NOTE The protection is offered to people's main residence, so vacation homes and rental property cannot claim an exemption.

Cars work the same way. Most states allow you to keep one vehicle. Most of the states allow between $1,000 and $2,000 in free value for your vehicle. It is not uncommon to see businesspeople at the end of their financial rope who still own cars and trucks free and clear. These people will be faced with the prospect of giving up their vehicle(s) or borrowing money from family members to pay the trustee the difference between the exemption amount and the value of the vehicle.

 NOTE The protection is normally offered to one vehicle per person, so if you own several cars (including cars used by your children), you stand to lose those extra cars, unless there are loans against them for more than their value.

I Will Lose All My Other Property

This is a constant fear of people. Much of what the bankruptcy lawyer does is define what property could possibly be taken by the bankruptcy court system and what cannot. Most small businesspeople who file *personal* bankruptcy will lose none of their personal property as every state allows a bankruptcy filer to keep personal property (furniture, clothes, appliances, etc.) with which to "get a fresh start". The great majority of our filers lose nothing.

However, there are exceptions. These normally come when the person who is filing has more property than the average person—an expensive house filled with fine furniture, business assets, several vehicles that are paid for, vacation or rental houses, collections that have a ready market, antiques, silver collections, expensive paintings, etc. What states allow people to keep is fairly bare-boned; extras and expensive extras are likely to be taken by the bankruptcy system.

They Will Sell My Property at an Auction in Front of My Home

The idea of not only losing one's property, but having it sold in a public way in front of one's neighbors, is horrifying. This almost never happens. The idea seems to come from seeing auctions of farm equipment as part of the TV news. Accounts of farmers' bankruptcies and the sale of their equipment are sometimes put on the air as news stories. These sales often happen at the farm. A farm is a business and the farm equipment and livestock have a high value and are hard to physically move. It makes economic sense to hold a sale where these items are located. The same is true of a store's inventory—although these sales often owe more to marketing hype than the bankruptcy process.

We have never seen a case where the trustee had household goods of such value that he or she would dream of having a sale at a person's house. It is far more effective to hold any sale of personal property at a central sales location where buyers are used to coming to purchase items. And of course, since the great majority of personal property is never taken and sold, there would be no sale in the first place.

It is possible, but unlikely, to have a home sold at public auction. This happens when a person files for bankruptcy, gives up his or her home, and the mortgages against it are so low that there will be something for the trustee to recover if he or she has an auction of the home. In such a case the trustee is likely to put ads in the newspaper saying a house at a given address will be sold at auction as part of the bankruptcy of "Joe Doe." The reason this does not happen in most cases is that people are careful to not file bankruptcy if they will run the risk of having their home taken from them by the trustee.

If I File, My Spouse Will Have to File Also

Small businesspeople often fear bankruptcy, because they worry about dragging their spouse into bankruptcy. They think that if one member of the marriage files, the other must also file. This is not correct. Bankruptcy is an individual process and one spouse files without the other all the time. However, spouses often find it makes sense to file together as both owe money to the same creditors. To have just one file in such a case would merely throw the debts back on the other.

In many cases, both spouses are not liable for the debts. One spouse may have operated the business and only one signed the loans. Or one of the spouses may have incurred the debts before the marriage, so the debts are only in that person's name. In such cases, one individual filing makes sense and is desirable. Having only one spouse file leaves the other spouse without debt and without a bankruptcy on his or her credit history.

But remember, while the debts are often in only one spouse's name, many of their assets are in both names. Make a careful examination of property owned and its value before a spouse files bankruptcy alone just as you would if you filed jointly.

My Spouse and I Will Lose Our Jobs

This is a real concern to people. Many small businesspeople run their business as a sideline to a day job—or have spouses who work. People do not automatically lose their jobs if they file bankruptcy and the employer learns of it. In fact, it is illegal to terminate someone because they filed for bankruptcy. Most employers never know that you filed for bankruptcy. Those who do know will often be glad you have addressed the financial problems that were disturbing you and causing you to receive collection phone calls at work. In addition, the employer may feel safer. Sometimes people embezzle money from employers in an effort to pay their debts. This temptation is gone if the debts have been addressed in bankruptcy.

It must be said, however, that there are some employers who do not look with favor on a bankruptcy filing. Normally these are employers in the financial industry. They are the ones who lose money because of bankruptcy and naturally do not look with favor on the process. Others are in the business of handling customers' money and feel it does not look good if one of their employees lets their personal finances get away from them.

I Will Lose My License

The government regulates many activities. They issue driver's licenses and licenses to engage in certain professions—barbers, insurance sales, doctors, contractors, and stockbrokers.

Some businesses involve licenses to handle other people's money—insurance sales, financial managers, and stock brokers. The majority of these people have not lost their licenses because of filing, and many have obtained licenses in some of these fields after bankruptcy. However, a blanket statement cannot be made, as these licenses are normally issued by the individual states and local governments. These rules can vary greatly from one local area to another. Many of these rules may require disclosure of a bankruptcy filing. Just to be safe, it is a good idea to ask about the licensing agency's policies before you file for bankruptcy.

I Cannot Get Student Loans

College and graduate school are very important. People often worry that they or their children will not be able to obtain student loans if they file bankruptcy. This fear is overblown. Loans for college and graduate school come from two sources. One is government-guaranteed student loan pools and the other is plain borrowing that is to be used to pay for schooling. Government-guaranteed student loans, the great majority of loans used for schooling, are not affected by a bankruptcy.

Borrowing from banks based solely on your credit is another matter. These loans, like any other loan, will be affected for several years until you rebuild your credit.

I Cannot Have a Bank Account

A person who is in bankruptcy or who has filed bankruptcy in the past is not prevented by law from having a checking or savings account with a bank or financial institution. Not being able to have a bank account is a common fear among people considering bankruptcy, and it is hard to see where the myth got started. Perhaps it arises from a garbled version of some real considerations concerning bank accounts in bankruptcy.

If people have a bank account with a bank they owe money to, it is often advisable to close that bank account or keep an amount of no more than a few dollars. This is because the banks who have money owed to them can freeze accounts and collect the money to pay off the debt owed to them. This is called the *right of off-set*. It means if I hold money for you, and you owe me money because of a debt, I can dip into the money I hold for you to satisfy the debt. For this reason people going through bankruptcy often close their bank accounts at the bank or credit union they have been doing business with.

The other possible source of the myth is that some people find it hard to open a new bank account after they have filed bankruptcy. Banks do not have to do business with you and some choose to not deal with people who have filed bankruptcy. However, banking is a competitive business and people can normally find a bank to deal with after their filing—they just have to work a little harder and perhaps go to a bank location that is less convenient for them.

I Will Be Put in Jail if I Do not Pay My Bills

Fear of jail or arrest because a bill is not paid is not unusual among people who cannot pay their debts. Bill collectors often play on this fear by threatening that they will send the sheriff out to see the debtor if the bill is not paid. Rest assured no one is ever put in jail for simply owing money. This might have happened hundreds of years ago, but not in the modern United States. Debt is what is called a civil matter—it is between two people or businesses and does not involve the government. It is not a breach of government rules (such as murder or robbery) that allows the government to jail a person.

The Debts Will Go Away in Time

If you cannot be jailed for debt, why file bankruptcy at all? After all, debts show up on your credit report for only seven years and you do not own anything of value—why even consider bankruptcy?

If you own little property, you are what lawyers call *judgment proof*. That is, a judgment can be taken against you, but there is nothing to collect against. Some states allow wage garnishment to collect on a private civil debt, but some do not.

This being the case, particularly if you live in a non-garnishment state or have irregular income, why worry about the debts? There are a couple of reasons.

- The debt removed from your credit report does not mean you no longer owe the debt. The obligation to pay a debt can easily last longer than seven years.

- The creditor can obtain a judgment against you. This has several effects. It will extend the time the obligation shows up on your credit report and will extend the life of the obligation.

- The judgment becomes a *judgment lien*. If you should acquire a home or land in the locale where the judgment is docketed, the judgment will attach itself against your real property. When you go to transfer the property the buyer will normally require that the judgment plus interest be paid. In this way the debt and judgment limit your ability to get back on your feet and move ahead. Judgment liens do not go away for a long time, and in fact, as your land or home becomes more valuable, may allow the creditor to seize the property.

A creditor obtaining a judgment starts the seven-year credit report clock running again. The applicable time period on your credit report is not just seven years from the original debt, but seven years from the last major debt activity.

I Can Never Have Credit Again

Simply put, this is not true. It may take some time and effort on your part, but you can have access to credit again. Section 19 covers this subject in detail.

Section 7

Alternatives to Bankrupting the Business or Yourself

Most people go through four different stages as they face financial hard times and before they consider filing for bankruptcy.

1. They try to lower their expenses or borrow additional funds to tide them over.
2. They attempt to deal with collection efforts by explaining their situation to the creditors and collector(s) and try to work with the creditors to arrange lower payments.
3. They consider a credit service that will attempt to work with their creditors for them.
4. They talk with a bankruptcy lawyer.

This is a logical sequence of responses, but people often tend to rush through some stages and spend too much time in others.

Working with business creditors is much the same as working with personal creditors, but there is one key difference: you are also a customer as well as a debtor to your suppliers as a business person. For this reason you are likely to be dealt with more gently than by a consumer debt collection agent who is collecting on an account they bought.

Budget

Stage one is a particular problem for small businesspeople. They often are faced with trying to trim business expenses and personal expenses at the same time. This is often done without drawing up detailed budgets for either their business or personal accounts.

This is a huge mistake. The importance of budgets cannot be overstated. The income of many small businesses will vary from month to month but this should not preclude making a budget for expenses. Expenses also vary from month to month with taxes, insurance and heat being higher in some months than others. But by going over several months' or years' bills, you can develop a monthly average. This will form the basis for your future decisions and calculations. Appendix A has some typical household and business categories that you can use as a template for developing your budget.

With a budget set out you can make decisions on where to cut spending. On the personal side you will find that there are only a few places you can cut. Food, clothing, and entertainment are typically the first to be cut. Items like house and car payments, on the other hand, are fixed and are missed only at the risk of causing severe problems.

NOTE If you are to the point where you are skipping house or car payments or are not paying taxes, you have severe problems and are likely beyond making simple expense adjustments.

Similar considerations hold true on the business side. Some expenses will be fixed—yellow page ads, phone, rent, and tool payments. Others can be varied—newspaper ads, bonuses, or your draw.

Borrowing and Debt Consolidation

Your house

We often see many people, both business people and individual employees, who have lost their homes or are four to eight months behind on their house payments. When asked how they got so far behind, many tell the same story: They were working on getting a loan on their house to refinance it and the loan never came through, or when it came through it was much more expensive than they had been told. Often people are presented with these higher interest rates and high closing fee loans when they go to closing. At that time they have no choice but to take the loan; they are months behind on their original loan and the creditors want all of their money in one lump payment right away. The people must either take the new high cost loan or lose their house.

These people have been the victims of unscrupulous loan brokers. There is a great deal of money to be made by matching up a lender and a borrower. Of course, this money can only be made if a borrower will wait around while the broker tries different lenders. Sometimes a match is made right away; sometimes it takes a long time. If it does take a long time it is very important to the broker to keep the borrower available. Some unscrupulous brokers get business by promising everyone who calls them that there is a very good chance they will get the loan. This gets the borrower tied in with them. Then they tell all types of stories about missing papers, people out sick, etc., to keep the borrower from trying something else.

Before you borrow against your home, keep these simple facts in mind.

1. Do not borrow against your house to pay credit card or other unsecured debts. Most people do not solve their debt problems by doing this. After all, their house payments go up and they are exchanging debt that a lawyer or Consumer Credit Counseling can do something about for a house mortgage that no one can do anything about. *You must pay every cent on time or you will lose your house.*

2. It normally takes about a week or two after you provide your information to know whether or not you got the loan. Never wait more than thirty days to find out about a loan. If you wait longer than that, see a lawyer or Consumer Credit Counseling at once.

Warning

If your house is being foreclosed on, see an attorney at once. You do not have time to get, and probably cannot afford, a refinanced loan. Do not pay any attention to a loan broker who tells you not to worry about the foreclosure or the about foreclosure served on you. The loan

(continued)

broker may not be able to take care of the problem. Too many people who have lost their homes or are within a day or two of losing their home while waiting for someone who told him or her not to worry. It does not matter to a broker if you lose your house, but he or she may make money off of you if you stick around during delays in your processing.

3. Do not pay any attention to how nice brokers are. They are always nice. The real test is: Did they get you the loan in a reasonable period of time? If not, see a lawyer or Consumer Credit Counseling about your money problems.

Disadvantages to borrowing against your home..

It is a high-risk gamble to borrow against your home to pay off other debts. It sounds so logical. Replace your many high interest rate credit card payments with one low tax deductible payment.

Keep in mind what you are doing.

- You are making a bet. If you lose the bet you lose your home. The bet is that you will not have any more credit card debt after you refinance your house. Many of the people who refinance to pay off credit cards go back and charge on their cards. Now they have two debts, a big house payment and credit card payments on top of that.
- You are betting nothing bad will happen to you. You assume you will not have a drop in income, you or your family will not get sick (and miss work), or you will not have big medical bills. You assume you and your mate will not split up or that you will not have to take on the care of a parent, a child or a grandchild. If one of these happens and you are "maxed out" on your home debt because of refinancing, then you are in danger of losing your home.
- You have exchanged a debt that would be paid off in the short term by making maximum payments for one you are likely to be paying for twenty-five or thirty years.

- You have exchanged a debt that a bankruptcy lawyer or Consumer Credit Counseling can do something about for one which cannot be modified.

Your retirement fund

Another thing many people do when they have financial problems is borrow against their retirement money. This is a terrible idea.

Something can be done about most debts, even houses that are being foreclosed on, but once your retirement money is gone it is gone. Social Security will not be enough to retire on. If you spend your retirement money you will not be able to retire and you will have to work when you are older. There are not many jobs for older people. This is why one sees so many senior citizens supplementing their incomes with jobs that teenagers used to do, such as bagging groceries and working at fast food restaurants. You may think your children will help you, but your kids may have problems of their own.

Hold on to your retirement money. Before you even think about taking money out of your retirement account because of money problems, see a bankruptcy lawyer or Consumer Credit Counseling.

Consolidating

Many people feel that if they could just get a debt consolidation loan they could come through their financial crisis. The idea of exchanging many payments for one is a seductive one. Unfortunately, this is seldom the answer to people's financial problems.

Financial institutions are often reluctant to loan money to people who are having financial problems because of a drop in income. They will look at a potential borrower's cash flow to see if the monthly loan payment can be made. Far too often there is little or no income to make the loan payments.

They will also look at the potential borrower's *debt to income ratio* (a number computed by dividing your income by your debt). If you already have high debts a lender is unlikely to give you money so you can pay off other lenders.

Even if you can obtain a debt consolidation loan while you are experiencing a financial crisis, you are likely to be charged a high interest rate. This will make paying off a new loan harder and it will take longer. In addition, the higher interest rate will mean your total monthly payments on the one loan is unlikely to be smaller than the sum of your other loans.

Dealing with Creditors

As noted in Section 3, dealing with creditors can be one of the worst experiences of your life. They are all too often rude, threatening and abusive. On the personal side, people often attempt to explain why they are not able to pay their bills and make arrangements to make partial payments. They often go so far as to call all their creditors and carefully and logically explain their situation and often to try and make partial payments for a while. Often this is a waste of time and emotional energy.

The collection process typically relies on teams of collectors working accounts. You may have a long conversation with "Joe" and work something out, and two days later "Sue" will call and deny any knowledge of this arrangement, insult you and demand payment in full.

Even if you are dealing with one creditor, your sincere efforts to explain yourself are not likely to work. Even the most kind-hearted collection agents become hardened after a while. They are lied to often and hear false promises from many debtors. In addition, the collection process demands results of the collection workers, and the system seems to have concluded that being rude and unreasonable is more cost-effective than being understanding and taking reduced payments. Thus you may be able, through great effort, to work out something with a few creditors, but the odds of getting all of your creditors to work with you are low.

Trade Creditors

Discussions with *trade creditors* are likely to be more fruitful. Most trade creditors will continue to sell to you on a C.O.D. basis, even if you run into payment problems with them. Selling to businesses is a competitive business and most sellers know that you have other vendors you can go to if they become too harsh.

Workout Program

The next step businesspeople typically try is a *workout program* brokered by a third party. There are very few groups that do this type of activity for business debts for very small businesses. There is really not much need since trade creditors tend to deal with you in a logical and businesslike manner.

On the other hand, there is a great need for such third parties when it comes to dealing with personal debt, as collectors on consumer accounts are very aggressive and hard to work with.

There are basically two types of intermediaries to use: Consumer Credit Counseling (CCC) and the "Not-for-Profit" ones that one often sees and hears advertised on T.V. or the radio.

Consumer Credit Counseling

CCC is a non-profit organization, often affiliated with The United Way, which is supported in part by the credit industry. Typically you go into their offices and meet face to face with a counselor. The charge to you is very low, and much of the financial support for CCC comes from the credit industry and The United Way. The value is high because the counselor, at your individual session, will go over your budget and analyze your debt status.

One great value of CCC is they will help you look at your personal budget and see what can be changed. CCC will normally set you up on a repayment plan that lasts about three to five years, and you will pay back all of the debt plus interest. Often a notation that you were in a CCC program will go on your credit report, but this is probably less damaging to your credit than many late payments, foreclosures, repossessions or bankruptcy.

Other Workout Programs

There are a growing number of other third party intermediaries. They often go by the names of debt counselors or debt consolidation agencies. Their infomercials and ads are common on TV and radio. These are typically labeled in their advertisements as a non-profit company. But, one must understand what is meant by *non-profit*. The term non-profit does not mean they do not make money. They often make very good money and their employees can earn a high salary. The term means that no profits are paid out (it is all spent on operating costs and salaries) or there are no shareholders who are entitled to profits. These companies typically make their money by charging you a handling fee. Or, they obtain an agreement with the creditor to let them have part of the money collected in exchange for collecting monthly payments from you and sending them to the creditors.

They say they will work out a deal with your creditors where you make one payment to them as debt adjustor and they will in turn pay your creditors. Unlike lawyers or the Credit Bureau, many of these operators are not licensed or regulated, so there are no limits on what they can do.

A few merely take your money and do not send it to anyone, so after months of faithfully making your payments you are out your money and still have the debts. Many are able to make arrangements with some, but not all, of your creditors. This means some creditors will still be calling you. Others may take your money and make minimum payments to your creditors—after taking a cut for themselves. At the rate they make payments for you it could be many years before your debts are paid off.

WARNING

Be very careful of anyone who does not have a local office you can go to. Go to that office before you send them any of your money. Find out if they are regulated by your state or are a United Way Agency. If not, be careful dealing with them.

If you use such a service, you should track what is happening to your loans very carefully. All too often people think things are going fine. They are making their monthly payments and the phone calls from creditors have largely stopped. It is only after several months that they learn their loan balances have not gone down. Ask specifically how long the payments will take to pay off your debt, because they are charging you each month and the organization may have an incentive to keep you in the plan as long as possible. You may want to read an expose of the industry titled "Pushed off the Financial Cliff" published in the July, 2001 issue of *Consumer Reports* (page 20) before signing up with a "not-for-profit" credit service other than Consumer Credit Counseling.

This article pointed out that some of the new third party intermediaries appear to be more interested in their own financial well-being than that of the debtors. One company was tied in with a lending company and hired a for-profit company owned by the intermediary's founder to do paperwork for the intermediary. This would mean that, while the credit counseling intermediary was technically not-for-profit, another organization was making a profit—and that company had personal ties with the principals of the credit counselors. The expose also noted that one intermediary kept the first payment to it for its fees, causing the debtor to be hit with late fees by his creditors, which the plan was supposed to pay.

Section 8
Lawyers,
Business Creditors,
and
Their Functions

Lawyers are often given a bad reputation. Many times to an outsider, it seems that what the lawyers are doing are routine actions that could be done by anyone with a little common sense. At other times it seems that the lawyers are making the whole process unduly complicated. Like many stereotypes there are some elements of truth in these claims—and much that is not true.

There is an old story about a factory owner whose key machine broke down and the whole plant could not run. The company repair people could not fix the problem and at last, in desperation, called in an outside mechanic. The mechanic said it would cost $500 to do a diagnostic and fix the machine, and the owner desperately agreed. The mechanic looked at the machine a few minutes and then opened the machine and replaced a belt and toggle switch. He then presented his bill. The owner was indignant, saying "$500 for those simple steps is outrageous," he said as he paid. "I could have done that." The mechanic said, "You are not paying for the replacement work, but for my knowing which belt and switch to replace. Besides, your factory is up and running again with a minimum of loss, so you have saved thousands of dollars."

That is what you are paying for when you hire a lawyer to work on your business financial issues. You are not paying him or her just to fill out forms, but for the knowledge of what will and what will not work in a complicated system.

The bankruptcy system is complicated partly because the laws often use compromising language that no one fully realized would produce the results it did. This wording is then thought about by smart people who examine every word and its relationship to others.

The lawyers who do bankruptcy cases everyday live in the world of this bankruptcy speak—they know what reasonable means in their courts and just how fair market value is deduced. They know where the system of conflicting men and women can be pushed and where it cannot. Much of the paperwork is routine. That is why it is possible in a simple case to do your own filing. But often business cases are not simple and that is why lawyers have a larger place in business bankruptcies. You, the client and consumer, also have a place, and you can benefit greatly by understanding in a general way what is going on. The lawyer may know the law and the local court customs, but you know your personal fact situation far better than the lawyer ever will. The lawyer uses questions and forms to try to collect all the pertinent facts, but these systems have flaws. He or she knows exactly what he or she means when asking you how many mortgages you have against your home. But you must know that a line of credit secured by your house is considered a mortgage to answer this question correctly.

It is suggested that when you start to have cash flow problems you see a lawyer fairly early in the process. If you have carefully read this book you will know some of the major traps to avoid as you work to save your business and your personal finances. There may be others that are specific to your situation that the lawyer can help with.

Workouts

A major step in saving any business is the workout. You and the lawyer, if you use one, are likely to be more successful if the creditor knows you understand your rights in these negotiations. The end game is bankruptcy. The creditor will (or should know that it will) receive little or nothing if you should have to file bankruptcy. Because of this, it is sometimes possible for the creditor to become something like a partner as you both work to find a way to avoid the catastrophe to each of you involved in bankruptcy.

First you must know who it is worth dealing with. Consumer debt—medical bills, credit cards, etc.—are not good candidates for work outs. From the creditor's point of view the amounts involved are fairly small. The credit industry seems to have made a calculation that it is more cost-effective to have some debtors go bankrupt than to undergo the expense of hiring people to spend time trying to resolve the debt crisis.

Business debts are very different. To a businessperson creditor, often a small business operation like yourself, your debt may be a major one to him or her. And if he can keep you alive on a reasonable basis, you represent future sales to him or her.

At first he or she may not appreciate the gravity of the situation and will often treat your protestations of money problems with a grain of salt. Creditors hear this type of thing all the time. They are likely to tell you that you must pay in full at once with no excuses.

However, the dynamics often change when a lawyer is brought in and starts explaining the ramifications of the problems. Spending money to have a lawyer shows that you are serious and that you have a serious problem—a problem that could result in business death for your company and losses for him.

What will often follow is a dance where your lawyer tries to secure breathing room and a continued flow of supplies for you. The business creditor, on the other hand, will try to secure a more protected position should your business fail and have to file bankruptcy.

COD

A common early step is to place your business on Cash on Delivery (COD). You receive your products and the seller is sure to receive money for goods sold right when he or she delivers them. This puts you in a tight position, but a surprising number of small businesses can live with this procedure. Furthermore, it at least allows them to continue to operate while they address their outstanding debts. This COD solution is such a reflexive step by the creditor that it is often an early warning sign that your financial problems are getting out of hand.

Many times a business cannot survive if it is placed on COD. Its *lead time* between goods received and service on products sold is too long. The business needs continued credit to continue to operate.

Liens

Sellers who know you are in trouble, and who may even have collectibles from you that are not being paid are understandably reluctant to give you more credit. Your only hope is to offer the seller an improved position in the event you file bankruptcy. What you can offer will depend on your business and what you have already given other creditors. A possible item is a *lien* on your accounts receivable, business equipment, or inventory. This type of action is a fine line for most small businesses to walk. Often they will not have inventory to offer, and equipment may already have a lien on it. Often the creditor does not want to risk taking an interest in your collectibles or equipment because it is not really set up to dispose of them.

Advantages and Possibilities of the Work Out

Another possible advantage of a work out guided by a lawyer or other third party is to simply get your creditor off your back. Receiving demanding phone calls from creditors saps your time and energy. Dealing with them takes time away from what could be spent on saving the business. Quite often a phone conversation with a third party who can unemotionally explain the consequences to everyone if your business fails will cause business creditors to back off. They must get something, but if a reasonable case can be made that a little time will allow the business to survive, they may stop the calls and lawsuits.

For a work out to be accepted you must have a brighter future. A job in the process of being done, a customer almost landed, and an improved economic prospect are all examples of what to present. Entrepreneurs by nature are optimistic. The first person you should try to convince is the lawyer you visit. They will tell you whether or not your plan or prospects make sense. Since the business is not their business they can be more objective about its prospects. While they are objective, they do not know as much about your business and your industry as you do, so it is possible to bluff on the truth with them. You are paying them good money for their advice and time so try to be as honest and objective as you can in telling them the facts of your situation.

NOTE Sometimes the mere mention of bankruptcy will be enough to make the creditors back off a bit and offer compromises. Sometimes it is the mention of bankruptcy by a lawyer that will do it. Other times nothing will stop the creditors and a work out is impossible. You cannot know until you start the process. If a work out is impossible then you will need to consider what will happen if you file bankruptcy.

Section 9
Traps and Mistakes to Avoid when You Have Money Problems

The businessperson should be thinking about what he or she will do if a business down-turn continues too long. In financial affairs, the ultimate retreat is bankruptcy. You want to fight as hard as you can to keep your business and personal finances going, but do so in a way that will leave you an exit strategy if that ultimately becomes necessary.

There are a number of classic mistakes people make when they are facing financial problems—mistakes that make it very hard to salvage their assets when they must consider bankruptcy. Some of the mistakes to avoid are:

- borrowing against a pension plan;
- borrowing against a home to pay off credit cards;
- borrowing from family and giving vehicle or home as security;
- taking cash advances on a credit card or cashing checks;
- living off of credit cards;
- transferring balances from one card to another;
- lying or puffing on loan applications;
- not paying income taxes;
- stopping payment of withholding taxes; or,
- not following corporate formalities.

Pension Plan Borrowing

One of the worst mistakes a person can make is to borrow against his IRA, 401K or other retirement account. It is so tempting. You need money and there is a ready source of funds, often quite large, sitting there just waiting for you to draw on it. The program even has a hardship withdrawal provision.

The problem with this course of action is how these withdrawals are treated for tax purposes and in bankruptcy. Retirement investments and savings are given tax-favored treatment because the government wants to encourage savings for people's old age. Further, there are tax penalties for taking the money out too soon. This is why you receive so little of the money if you simply cash out your retirement account. Taxes eat up a huge portion of the money you draw out. To avoid this tax you must set up a repayment program.

However, under bankruptcy, retirement loan repayments are treated as payments to yourself and are not considered as a living expense when computing what you can afford to pay towards your debts. This presents a *Hobson's choice* to the person who has borrowed against his or her retirement savings. When the court calculates income to determine what type of bankruptcy the person must do (Chapter 7 or Chapter 13), the available money is higher by this payment and is setting the level of the Chapter 13 payment that money is counted as money that can be taken to repay debts. However, if bankruptcy takes this money the retirement loan cannot be paid back. A huge tax liability is triggered by a premature withdrawal from the retirement account. It is an impossible problem. It is better to leave the money in your retirement account and never borrow against it than face this problem.

Borrowing against a Home to Pay Off Credit Cards

A close second to borrowing against your retirement account is borrowing against your home to pay off credit cards. The ads are so seductive: "Pay off your high interest credit cards with a lower interest second (or third or fourth) loan against your home. The interest payments may even be tax deductible." This is so seductive that more and more people are taking this very step. This can be a big mistake.

Primarily, you are trading debts you can discharge in bankruptcy for a debt you must pay to avoid losing your home.

However, sometimes it can be a good idea. A person's home is the queen of his or her property. Almost everyone who is considering bankruptcy says first, "I don't care what else I lose, I want to save my home." A house is more than shelter for one's family. Although that is very important, it is the receptacle for one's dreams and often how one defines oneself to the world. In fact, one of the reasons people do not look into bankruptcy sooner is a general feeling that one loses one's home when one files bankruptcy.

This often does not happen, but it can. To avoid losing your home, planning on borrowing can be very important. Almost every state allows a person to keep a home if they do not have too much equity in the house (the value of the house less what is owed on it). How much equity you can have will vary by state. In New York it is $10,000. In New Jersey there is no state exemption but one can use the federal exemption of $16,150. In California it can range from $50,000 to $125,000 depending on your age and marital status. Some states, notably Florida and Texas, allow unlimited exemptions (but do limit the size of the property).

If you have equity in your home over the allowed maximum, you run the risk of losing your home. The trustee can sell it, give you the protected equity, and distribute the balance of sale proceeds to your creditors. The trustee will typically give you the chance to buy the house first at what he would likely receive from the sale, but you normally cannot come up with a large amount of money when filing bankruptcy.

One way to avoid the problem is to have more debt on your home. Here is a place where it may make sense to borrow against your home in order to pay off your business and personal debts. If you can weather your financial storm by reducing your credit card payments, and move your house equity into the protected zone, this program of borrowing may make sense, but only in a planned logical way. To do this you need to know three things:

1. the home exemption in force in your state (You can get a general idea by looking at Appendix B, but do not rely on it. States change their exemption levels constantly and any printed book runs the risk of being out of date; check with a bankruptcy lawyer.);

2. how much you owe on your home (A simple call to your mortgage holder for the payoff will gather this information.); and,

3. the value of your home.

This third thing is not as simple as it seems. Most people, when asked for the value of their home, will give the value it was appraised at. Historically this made since, as banks wanted their appraisals to be concrete. Today lenders are more interested in having the loan go through. To do this they need a "good" house value. The lending industry is now putting pressure on appraisers to "push" the house values—to give it the highest plausible value.

The problem is that these artificially pushed values often are unrealistic when it comes to selling the house, particularly if the sale is to be soon after the appraisal. In your planning you might collect a realistic value for the house. Normally this is a blending of real estate agents' values (remember these also are often high), the appraisal and the tax values. It is well worth paying a bankruptcy lawyer to discuss with you what the local legal bankruptcy culture on house value is before making your borrowing plans. You may even want to hire your own appraiser and tell him or her to not artificially push the value. You are working with your most precious asset and you do not want to be flying blind when making your plans.

When you have these numbers it makes sense to borrow up to the line of your state exemption, and no further. If your state exemption is $10,000 and your home has $30,000 in equity, borrow $20,000 against your home and pay down other bills. This way you may weather your financial problems.

Be able to pay monthly installments

By all means *do* borrow against your house to pay back what you borrowed from your 401(K) or retirement plan. As noted above, loans from retirement programs hurt you if it comes to bankruptcy and loans against extra equity in your house, within limits, can help you save your home.

Within limits is a key term. It does not do you a bit of good to borrow against your home if you cannot make the monthly payments. Whether it is called a second mortgage or a home equity loan, it still has your house as collateral. As such you will lose your home to fore-closure if you do not make the monthly payments. (It is amazing how many businesspeople, when asked to list the mortgages against their home, will not list a home equity line. Somehow the difference in the name fools them.)

Borrowing from Family and Giving a Vehicle or Home as Security

After reviewing the problems of borrowing against a vehicle or a home, people often go to family and friends and borrow money. They give their car title or promise their home as security for the loan. The lender in a such friendly loan situation will either hold their car title or have their name listed as a lien holder on the title. If it is a loan against the home they will draw up a note themselves and note the home is the collateral for the loan. Such informal loans and security actions almost never hold up in bankruptcy court. The trustee sets aside the lender's claim and the vehicle or home is treated as if nothing was owed on it.

If someone is going to lend you money with your vehicle or home as security, take the time to put the transaction on a formal basis with the proper security documents. It is better to spend a little money to have a lawyer do the paperwork than to lose your vehicle or home. And remember, if the documents are not correct your family member may have to give back the loan payments you paid them because it is considered an insider preference.

Taking Cash Advance on a Credit Card or Cashing Checks

As money pressures mount, people often turn to what credit they can to gain funds to keep the business going and to live. Common sources are credit cards, large cash advances, or cashing the checks creditors often send to people in the mail. The problem with these is that this creates a spike in your borrowing pattern. There once was a time when if a creditor extended you credit and you were not able to repay it, that was the creditor's problem. But, over the years the credit card companies were able to convince courts that such debts should not be discharged.

Credit card companies started looking for anything that looked like a spending spree, such as a large charge in a short period of time. A large cash advance, or cashing a mailed check will be treated as the same burst of spending as a Las Vegas vacation. Often the credit cards will attack first and try to put the burden on you to demonstrate you were not trying to defraud them. This aggressive action by the credit card industry when you take cash advances or cash checks can make your bankruptcy more expensive as you may have to defend yourself in bankruptcy court, and you may even lose if the judge does not think you acted properly. The best advice is not to change your charging habits.

Living on Credit Cards

If you are using a credit card to tide you over the rough spots you should be reasonable. You must make a realistic assessment of when there is no hope of turning the business around, or making it go, or getting a job. If it goes to court or is challenged by the credit card company, the judge will make an assessment of your judgment and whether you should have thought you had a realistic chance of repaying the money you were borrowing on the credit card.

Transferring Balances from One Card to Another

Sometimes advice you are given about trying to work yourself out of debt can come back to harm you. One bit of advice one often hears is to move debt from a high interest credit card to a lower interest credit card. This helps by reducing the amount you must pay each month, and in theory makes it easier to pay off your debts.

The problem with this strategy in the bankruptcy context is that it creates the same type of spike on the new lower interest credit card that a cash advance or a Las Vegas trip would. And even though the credit card company encouraged you to take this action in their promotional literature, they may turn around and attack you for bankruptcy fraud. You will be faced with the expense and worry of responding to their claims and accusations.

Again, the best safeguard against this type of problem is sober judgement. You must step back and make an assessment as to whether or not making such a balance transfer will really help or whether you are merely rearranging the deck chairs on the Titanic.

Lie or "Puff-Up" Numbers on Loan Applications

Bankruptcy has a way of making small lies about your income or your assets on loan applications blow up in your face. For large loans you may have to produce income tax records, but often people are able to make a case that they are not accurate and have the loan officer accept the explanation. Or the potential borrower may give insurance, replacement value, or more for business equipment and personal items. Often this is done with their acquiescence or even the pushing of the loan officer. One story heard fairly often is that a finance company loan person will tell the would-be borrower, "You don't have enough asset value to qualify for the loan; think again about your goods and their value". Some even go through the application and systematically mark up the values given.

All of this blows up when a bankruptcy petition is filed. The income is lower and is not based on predictions but on cold depressing facts. The values of goods and property are listed at a far lower forced sale value. The relatively friendly and helpful loan officer disappears. In her place comes a stern recovery officer waving the loan application and implying fraud on the borrower. These differences can be very hard to explain even if the difference is the innocent *puffing-up of numbers* when applying for the loan. It can be far worse if you actually lied.

At best, loans made on the basis of your fraud are not dischargeable, and at worst you may face criminal charges of fraud. Never lie on a loan application. Always try to put a fair value on your assets and do not let the loan taker put down information that is not correct. The same set of statements are always made, "I didn't say (write) that," and, "That's your signature isn't it?"

Not Paying Income Taxes

When you are having money problems a seemingly easy source of money is the government. People simply do not pay their taxes. It takes every bit of money they have to stay afloat and at year end they have nothing to send the government. Small businesspeople are particularly susceptible to this, as they do not have wages from which to withhold.

This is a big mistake. The IRS may be acting nicer of late, but they are still a very hard organization to deal with. Taxes are a necessary, integral part of a business and if you cannot afford to pay them you should not be in business. It is possible to be opportunistic for a year and come up short at the end of the year. But the IRS will be much less sympathetic if you have several years of not paying your taxes than if you have one.

NOTE File a tax return even if you cannot pay your taxes for the year or do not believe you owe any because of low income or losses.

In certain cases it is possible to completely discharge taxes in bankruptcy. The rules are complex, but basically the taxes must be old ones and you must have filed your tax returns. If you do not file your return you are not eligible for this limited chance at complete discharge.

When it comes time to deal with your late taxes they will be much higher than the simple amount you owed for a given tax year. The IRS will add interest and penalties, which can be quite devastating.

Stopping Payment of Withholding

Closely allied to not paying your taxes is not paying money collected as sales taxes or as employee withholdings. Probably seventy-five percent of the businesses in financial trouble have taken this route. This is worse than not paying income tax. This type of tax liability cannot be discharged in bankruptcy. In addition, officers of the business are also liable for the taxes. This means if you made your wife or your daughter vice president or secretary, they are personally liable even if they had nothing to do with the operation of the business.

Not Following Corporate Formalities

One of the reasons to establish a corporation is to protect your personal property, house, cars, savings, etc. from claims of creditors. As noted above, these assets often are at risk because businesspeople are forced to sign personally as guarantees of corporate debts.

But, sometimes the corporate owner can avoid having his or her personal assets secure the business debts. This normally happens after the business has operated successfully for a few years. Lenders may stop requiring personal guarantees, and vendors may sell to the company and not the businesspeople. Then when the business slows down, these creditors have to start collection actions at once if they are to recover anything.

The organizers of the business are often careful to have the corporation formed and filed with the Secretary of State. This is what breathes life into the corporation. They are typically less careful to take the steps to keep the corporation alive. To do this you must mind the formalities of a corporation and this means having meetings, authorizing corporate action, and electing officers. In some corporations so little attention is paid to these formalities that organizational meetings are never held, thus creating a real question of whether or not the corporation was ever born. More common is to file with the state, hold the organizational meeting to elect directors and officers, and then put the corporate minutes book away and never take any of the actions necessary to keep the corporation alive.

This is a common temptation. You are busy running the corporation and you or your small group are the corporation. You know what you are doing, you do it, and that is that. It is very unnatural to sit down, put on a shareholder's hat, elect directors, and then put on a director's hat, approve your business actions and elect yourself as an officer. It seems like a silly formality at best and at worst like a witch doctor's ritual. And what is worse, to be done correctly it costs money to hire a lawyer to write up the documents.

But, these silly steps can be all important when a business creditor is trying to take your house for a business debt. How is this ever possible? The whole point of forming the corporation was to prevent such a thing from happening.

What the creditor will claim is that you did not have a real corporation—that the corporation is only your alter ego. You may have created the corporation but you let it die from neglect and after a while the corporation no longer existed—just you or your group running the business as a sole proprietorship or a partnership. This is called *piercing the corporate veil*. Do not let this happen to you. If you went to the trouble and expense of forming the corporation, go to the extra expense and trouble of keeping it alive by doing corporate minutes as you go along.

If a collecting creditor is talking about piercing the corporate veil, do not go back and draw up several years of records at one time. You will open yourself up to charges of fraud. You are far better working your way through the facts you have, than trying to work last minute changes.

Section 10

Analyzing Business Debts and Assets Before Bankruptcy

As was noted in Section 5, it is very common for the small businessperson to have large personal debts that are connected to or attributable to the business. Credit cards or personal loans may have been used to start the business or keep it going. Homes and vehicles may have been offered as security on these loans.

If you are considering bankruptcy for your business you must determine how much personal liability you have for business debts. This discussion will apply only to businesspeople that have formed corporations or limited liability companies in an effort to shield their personal assets from business debts. If one is operating as a sole proprietor then all business debts are personal debts. There are several classes of business debts discussed below.

Leases

Most businesses have a location they operate out of. It may be a storefront where they sell goods or meet customers. Or, it may be a space where they repair items or perform other services. For most small businesses, this space is leased. Business people typically think of this as an obligation of the business and that the obligation will go away if the business is shut down. This is often not true.

Most landlords know they will recover little or nothing for future missed lease rent if a business closes down. For this reason most leases are written so that an individual personally guarantees the lease. To see what you agreed to, carefully review your lease agreement to see if your name personally appears on the lease at the signature line. If it says the signer is "X Company by Tom Doe, President," or words to that effect, you *may not* have personally guaranteed the lease. However, if it merely has your name and your signature, you probably personally guaranteed the lease.

Vehicle and Equipment Leases

Vehicle and equipment leases will generally operate the same as real estate leases. Again, examine the document to see who are the signing parties.

Business Credit Cards

Today many business people carry credit cards with their business name on them. Many people think these are business credit cards and that money charged on them is debts of the business only. This is often not correct. The agreement signed with the credit card company should be checked to see if it was signed by you as an officer of the company or by you individually.

Purchase Agreements

Businesses need supplies and often these are bought on credit extended by the vendor. Sometimes the vendor will set up the account in the name of the corporation or limited liability company and sometimes in your personal name. Most businesspeople do not pay attention to how vendors' accounts are set up when they are starting their business and when times are good. But this simple fact can make a big difference when times turn bad and the businessperson must decide whether or not he or she will need to file bankruptcy and what debts should be listed.

If you do not have a copy of the vendor's contract, ask for it and then examine it to see who is listed as the contracting party. If there is not a formal contract, then examine the invoices sent to you. Often these will be used by the legal system to determine who are the parties to the agreement. Of course, all letters and memos between you and the vendor should be reviewed to see what light they can shed on who are the parties to the credit extension.

Another form of purchase agreement is when you have contracted to buy tools that you will need to use in your business. Often the sellers of tools extend credit to buyers to allow the purchase of expensive tools and equipment. Normally this credit is extended to the businessperson as an individual, but the contracts should be checked.

Assets

Almost every business has assets and often there is a great deal of confusion over whether or not a given asset is owned by the corporation or the individual. Some items such as vehicles are titled and it is a fairly straightforward matter to check the title to see who is listed as the owner. For other items it is harder. Computers, desks, typewriters, etc., are not titled and could belong to either the business or the individual. You should check tax records and maintenance agreements to see how they are listed. Also check the purchase agreements drawn up when you bought the item. Who is shown as the purchaser? Was a corporate or business check used to pay for the item? It is hard to argue a computer is your personal property if it was paid for by a corporate check using corporate money, the warranty agreement is in the business name, and it is listed as business property for tax purposes.

Value

Once you know who owns what, you should place a value on the property. If you file a personal bankruptcy, often what you lose or are allowed to keep will depend on the value of the goods. If the corporation owns the property and it files for bankruptcy, value does not matter because all corporate property will be taken.

Most people, when asked the value of their business or personal property, will list what they paid for it or what it would cost to replace the item. Sometimes they have no interest in selling the item and will place a high value on the item as it would take that much money to induce them to sell it. Other times people will list what they would sell the item for if they had time and found just the right buyer. These are approaches that will lead to problems in most bankruptcies.

What the businessperson should think about is how much the property would bring if it were sold in a fairly short period of time, or what one could get after making a reasonable effort to sell it. This should take into account the fact that the item is used and often not in the best of shape. This is often the value to the bankruptcy system.

You should consider how easy it is to sell the item. Some things, like vehicles and baseball cards, have a ready market. Other items, such as collectibles, may bring a good price if you traveled to another town to sell at a convention of collectors, but may bring almost nothing in your local town.

Vehicles are in a special class. There is a ready market for them and resale and market values are listed in books and on the Internet. Many people assume the value of a vehicle is what they can sell it for. This is not the case. The Supreme Court held that the value is what it would cost to buy the vehicle.

The holding of the case is open to different interpretations and different lower courts have come up with different ways of computing this replacement value. These range from the full purchase price, to ninety percent of the purchase price, to an average of the wholesale and the purchase price.

It is very hard for someone not used to dealing with the local bankruptcy court to come up with the value the court would use to value vehicles and other property. The best course of action is to draw up a list of your assets, work out both a replacement value and a sale value for them, and then talk to a lawyer to learn what value the court would use.

Profit and Loss

Most small businesspeople are in business because they have a skill they can sell, or an activity they enjoy doing. Many, if not most, of them do not have any background in bookkeeping and don't enjoy doing it. In fact, many avoid it because time spent keeping the books is time away from making money. They, at best, turn the record keeping over to a spouse or maybe a hired bookkeeper.

The result is chaos. Many small businesspeople, when asked for income, will give what the business on average earns or clears each month, without taking taxes into account. Taxes are something paid at the end of the year and are to be worried about then. Gas for vehicles is lumped in with gas for personal cars. The same problem comes up with food if their business involves overnight travel.

This approach to business and personal debts has been called the "cigar box method" of running a business. In the past, a business owner would keep a cigar box of cash by the cash register. When a sale was made the money went into the box. When a supplier needed to be paid the money came from the cigar box. If money was needed by the kids for school or for groceries, it came out of the box. Everything was fine as long as the box had money and no effort was made to differentiate between business expenses and personal expenses.

This will not work if you go into bankruptcy. Since bankruptcy is a personal matter, it is important to know how much the business is earning and what its expenses are, including taxes. When these are worked out an individual can see what he has available for living and can then work out what his personal living expenses are. Many small businesspeople are shocked to learn how little they are being paid for their long hours of hard work when they figure out their income and expenses.

Section 11

Taking a Financial Inventory

There are two steps to taking a financial inventory. The first is seeing how bad your debt situation really is. The second is classifying your debts and assets.

Computing Your Debt Ratio

After interviewing thousands of people over the years, we have developed a quick test to determine just how bad a person's debt situation is. For lack of a better name, we call it the *Quick Ratio*. It is the relationship between your take home pay and how much you owe, not counting your vehicle and house debt.

To work out your ratio do the following (using the form on page 79):

☛ Step One: Take your paychecks and work out how much money you have each month after taxes, insurance, and retirement are deducted. Money your employer is withholding for payments to a credit union for an unsecured debt and money you are putting into savings (stock purchase, Christmas Club, etc.) need to be added back in. This gives you your *net pay*.

NOTE If you and your spouse both work, compute net pay for both of you.

☛ Step Two: Multiply your monthly net pay by 12 to get your yearly take home income.

☛ Step Three: Add up the total of all your debts except what you owe on your house, vehicles, student loans, and taxes.

☛ Step Four: Divide your total short-term debt by your yearly income.

Quick Ratio Worksheet

1) My take home pay is   _____

2) Add back:
   a) Christmas account   _____
   b) Payment to credit union
      for signature loans   _____
   c) Money to savings account   _____
   d) Stock purchase   _____
   e) Savings program   _____

   Total   _____

3) If you are paying alimony, child support,
or criminal restitution out of your take home
pay, deduct these amounts   _____

4) a) If you are paid weekly multiply by 4.3   _____
   b) If you are paid every 2
      weeks multiply by 2.15   _____
   c) If you are paid 2 times a month
      multiply by 2   _____
   d) If you are paid monthly multiply by 1   _____
      Multiply your monthly income by 12   _____

5) My total short term debt (the actual debt; not
   just what you are paying each month)
   a) Medical bills   _____
   b) Money owed after repossessions   _____
   c) Credit cards   _____
   d) Bank loans   _____
   e) Department store debt   _____
   f) Finance company loans   _____
   g) Jewelry debt   _____
   h) Stereo and appliance debt   _____
   i) Loans from family & friends   _____

   Total   _____

6) Total from step 5   _____
   Divided by total from 4   _____

Quick Ratio is   _____

This quick test assumes you do not have unusually high housing, car, tax and student loan payments. It also assumes your medical expenses and gifts to the church are average. To get a very detailed debt to income ratio, all of these factors would need to be considered. But the Quick Ratio will give you a good starting point.

What the ratio means is:

- If the ratio is .15 or lower you are generally in good financial shape.
- If the ratio is .15 to .25 you are starting to get a little too much debt. You should cut back your spending and pay down your debt.
- If your Quick Ratio is over .25 you are showing signs of a dangerous debt situation. The larger the Quick Ratio the worse your situation (of course if your ratio is .26 you can fix up things easier than if it is a .65).

Generally speaking, people or couples whose ratio is between .35 and .85 are sinking deeper and deeper into debt. They may be able to make their minimum payments, but they are not taking care of the underlying debt. Even worse, they are slowly getting worse off. That is, if they add up their total debt from six months ago and their total debt today, today's debt is likely to be higher. Further, without some drastic action, the total debt six months in the future will be higher than it is today. Many people in this situation do not really realize the danger they are in and even think they have perfect credit. They are probably getting pre-approved credit applications in the mail.

However, people with this ratio rank are slowly sinking into debt. The fact that their total debt is getting larger means that they in effect are paying the monthly payments on their debt with borrowed money when all is said and done. As long as they can get borrowed money from their credit cards or other creditors, they can easily make timely payments. But, this cannot go on forever. Eventually even the most foolish creditors will stop making money available. Without more money to help live and pay the monthly payments, it becomes impossible to stay afloat and a financial crisis happens.

People whose Quick Ratio is above .9 are very close to the financial crisis if they are not already in it.

NOTE There are two ways to get a high Quick Ratio. One is to borrow more money either slowly or all at once. This increases the debt part of the equation. The other is to have a drop in personal or household income. This reduces the income part of the equation. If your household income is cut in half you can go from a safe Quick Ratio to a very bad one—overnight.

What should you do if your Quick Ratio is over .9? Make an appointment at once with a bankruptcy lawyer or call Consumer Credit Counseling. The phone number for Consumer Credit Counseling is listed in the business white pages of most phone books. You can also call the lawyer referral line of your state bar for a bankruptcy lawyer near you. These are normally located in your state capital. (Call information and ask for the lawyer referral service of the state bar.)

Classifying Your Debts and Assets

If your debt ratio is high, you should begin working out your mix of debts and assets in case you need to file bankruptcy. To gain a rough idea of how bankruptcy will effect you, you must first list and categorize your debts and assets. The bankruptcy court treats different debts in different ways, likewise, certain classes of assets come in for different treatment.

Debts

At its simplest, a *debt* is a promise to pay someone a sum of money; however in the modern world, this simple rule has been stretched and bent until a large number of items that are classified as debts must be dealt with in bankruptcy. The two main divisions are: (1) secured debts versus unsecured and (2) contingent debts versus present debts.

Secured debts

A *secured debt* is one where property can be taken by the creditor if the debt is not paid. The classic examples are car and house loans. If you do not pay these debts, the creditor can repossess the car or foreclose on the home. These simple concepts can be tricky. A surprising number of people feel that loans from finance companies where the finance company holds the car title is not a secured car loan. They feel that since they paid off the original financing of the purchase of the car arranged with the dealer and the bank, that they do not have a car loan anymore. A loan from a finance company who holds your car title is almost always a secured loan and they can repossess your car just as fast as the bank that did the original financing.

Likewise, many people do not consider home equity loans, or lines of credit secured by a home to be mortgages. They are both secured by the home and if they are not paid in a timely way the holder can foreclose on the home.

Jewelry or electronics bought with the selling company's card are often secured. A merchant company's credit card often has clauses in the contract that make it different from a true credit card. But, because they are both plastic and the same shape, people often believe both are unsecured credit card debts. Businesspeople often secure loans from creditors with company assets, inventory, equipment, or tools.

Unsecured debts

Unsecured debts are, by definition, debts without property pledged as security for the repayment of the debt. Examples are major credit cards such as Visa®, Master Card® and American Express®. Medical debts, signature loans, and utility bills are other examples of unsecured debts. If you owe money on a car that has been repossessed and sold, that debt is unsecured—there is nothing more they can take from you.

Some credit card companies send credit solicitations to small businesspeople with offers for "company credit cards" or "business account cards." When issued, the business name is written in large letters on the cards. Credit card companies offer the chance to charge business expenses on the card. Often they tout the value of having all your business expenses listed on one account for ease of record keeping. They may even list the advantage of earning free travel miles on your charges. The implication is that you can earn travel mileage points for airline travel on tax-deductible business expenses. Some also stress that you can use their card for working capital.

Many businesspeople naturally think charges on theses cards are company debts and they are not personally responsible for the charges on the cards. This can be a serious mistake. You should examine closely the solicitation form you filled out and sent in when you signed up for the card (or the signature portion of the solicitation you are considering signing up for). Most of the time it will call for your individual signature and often your social security number. These are indications that they are issuing the card to you as an individual. They need your social security number to check your credit history before deciding whether or not to issue you the individual credit card. The company name on the card is merely to appeal to your ego, and what little advantage you get in record keeping and earning travel miles or business expenses. The emphasis behind it is in marketing cards via affinity, the way clubs and colleges have an affinity card. Money owed on these "business credit cards" should be counted as personal unsecured debt when you are taking your financial inventory.

Sometimes debts that appear secured are treated as unsecured in bankruptcy. Often finance companies, when they make you a loan, have you list property you already own as security—T.V.'s, furniture, etc. In bankruptcy these "non purchase security items" can often be protected by filing a special motion. The test is: are they items you already owned and used to operate your household? What is considered a *household good* will vary from state to state. Often sports equipment such as golf or tennis equipment are not considered necessary to operate a household and are not within this exemption. Firearms are often treated differently from state to state.

Contingent Debts

The *contingent debts* are those that are dependent on an event that has not yet happened. A straightforward example is being a *codebtor* on a loan. You will not owe the money unless the main borrower defaults. Another type is the so called *unliquidated debt*. This is when you may or may not owe the debt. This normally arises in a car accident where you are being sued by a person who says the accident and the damages were your fault. You dispute this claim. You do not owe him or her anything until the court rules against you and sets a dollar amount you are to pay.

Other debt types

There are several other types of debts covered on bankruptcy forms.

Unmatured Debts: The event creating the duty to pay has not yet occurred. For example, you borrowed money and gave a promise to pay it back in three years. Until that three years has passed you have only future liability and the debt is unmatured. After the three years have passed, the debt becomes matured. This is a form of contingent debt.

Disputed Debts: This is another form of contingent debt. This is a debt a third party claims you owe him or her, but which you deny. There are several situations where this can arise. You hire someone to do work for you and they do a bad job. They claim payment and you deny you owe them that much, or perhaps nothing, because of the poor quality of the work. Another common situation is where you have paid the debt and the creditor claims they never got the money. They may still be trying to collect, or the claim may only be on your credit report. Another situation is where you never bought anything from the creditor, but he or she claims you owe money and are trying to collect on it or are listing it on your credit report.

Co-signed debts

Some debts are debt where you and another person have both signed for a loan. You are both liable. It does not make any difference whose name is first on the loan. You are each liable for the entire debt. Many people believe since there are two or three signers, they are only liable for one half or one third of the debt. This is not true. Each person can be sued for the entire debt. It is completely up to the creditor who the company goes after for the money.

Taxes, student loans, alimony and child support

Debts are also classified by who is owed the money. The most common are taxes, student loans, alimony, child support, and criminal fines.

Taxes: These are debts owed to a government entity—federal, state or local. These debts may or may not be dischargeable depending on the type of tax and how old it is. Some taxes cannot be discharged in bankruptcy at all. Two examples are withholding taxes and sales taxes. Back income taxes may be discharged if they are old enough and certain other conditions are met.

Student loans: At one time student loans, if they were old enough, could be discharged in bankruptcy. Congress has ended this exemption. Now, except for cases of extreme hardship, student loans cannot be wiped out in bankruptcy. Owing a lot of money and having no funds is not extreme hardship. This is the situation of almost everyone in the bankruptcy courts. What *is* hardship is decided by a judge in each case, so results vary. It often involves a new sickness or disability that would prevent you from ever making the income necessary to repay the loan.

Alimony: Occasionally people come to us with the bright idea of wiping out their duty to pay alimony in bankruptcy. It cannot be done. In fact, alimony is so protected in the bankruptcy procedure that some regular debts are deemed alimony and are protected from bankruptcy discharge. It works like this: Often in the past a person, in separation or divorce papers, would agree to pay certain debts owed by both spouses. Many times this was in exchange for not paying alimony. The trade off was,"I will pay the debts so I cannot afford to pay alimony." The person would then file bankruptcy and thus end up without alimony or debts. The spouse would end up with no alimony and would be liable on the joint debts.

Congress put a stop to this by saying that such debts were to be treated as a form of alimony and cannot be discharged if the spouse objects to the debt being wiped out. This system does not prevent a person from trying to wipe out these debts and puts the burden on the spouse to object.

Child support: This simply cannot be wiped out in bankruptcy.

Criminal fines and court-ordered restitution: These cannot be wiped out in bankruptcy. In fact, the bankruptcy court has remarkably little power to interfere with what a criminal court is doing.

Assets

Home

The average person's most important asset is his or her home, both in monetary value and in psychological terms. The biggest worry people always have is, "Will I loose my home?" Normally they will not. If you look at the exemption charts in Appendix B, you will see the value of a home that can be protected is normally quite small. Ten to thirty thousand dollars is the normal range. However, this is *equity value*, the difference between the *market value* (what you could sell it for) and what is owed on it in first, second, and third mortgages. As long as your home equity is within the protected range, your home is safe.

Three problems can arise in this simple equation. One—many people have trouble determining the market value of their home. They first, naturally enough, give the value the appraiser used for the mortgage on their home. Unfortunately this is not always a true market value. Many lenders are now putting pressure on appraisers to "push" the appraised value. That is, they want appraisers to give an appraisal figure that is the highest supportable value.

The higher the appraisal, the more likely the loan will go through. After all, lenders do not make money, and their employees do not earn salaries, unless loans are made. It may be that the mortgage industry is gambling that it will never have to try to recoup loaned money by actually selling the homes that secure loans.

Since you cannot depend on appraised value, estimates and averages are the next best thing. Many areas are using tax value. Historically, tax values of homes were lower than the true market value of the property. That is not always the case today. Some taxing authorities have found they can raise more taxes by having a higher tax appraisal on the homes and other property in its jurisdiction. People generally like being told their homes are worth more, and those who object to the increased value (and the higher taxes it produces) are often too busy to go through the laborious process of protesting the higher assessed value. Thus over time, tax value has moved closer to actual value.

Two—another source of information is a real estate agent. It may be possible to have a real estate agent give you an idea of what your house would sell for. Just be aware that many real estate people are by nature optimistic. They may also "push" the value of the house to some degree.

Three—if in doubt, you can always pay to have an appraisal done by your own appraiser. This is not fool-proof. The appraiser can be wrong about the value. Some people think they will hire a "friendly" appraiser and get a low value appraisal for their home. This is a mistake.

A trustee can question the appraiser's value, leading to a trial and great expenses. But having a fair appraisal does give you another source of information about your most valuable asset.

The bigger problem comes when a home does not have a mortgage on it, either because the mortgage has been paid off (as often happens with older people) or because the mortgage is no good. This does not happen often, but occasionally the mortgage will have a technical flaw. The property description may be wrong, it may be recorded in the wrong county, or even not properly signed.

If any of these things happen, the value of the asset is likely to be far higher than the relatively low protection value for homes allowed by most states.

Other real estate

This category can cover vacation homes, time shares, and investment property (such as rental homes, second homes, and homes owned for family members to live in). This property, not being the place where the filer calls home and lives, is generally not protected by federal or state exemptions.

Vehicles

These can be either personal or company cars. As with houses, the exemption for these in most states is quite low. Therefore, if the vehicle is owned outright, and is fairly new, it may be lost in bankruptcy.

People are often surprised by how high the value is on their vehicles in the bankruptcy system. When they seek to sell the vehicle or to borrow money against it they are faced with a far lower value. The reason for this difference is that in bankruptcy the value is *replacement value*. Thus the courts look to see what a dealer would charge you if you bought the vehicle from it.

Rented or leased personal property

Leased property, vehicle leases, or rent to own property such as televisions, stereo systems, and furniture, are not uncommon. The right to use the property is an asset, but is normally not one that would be lost in bankruptcy.

Personal household goods

This includes items such as furniture, clothes, jewelry, books, musical instruments, etc. This is the most elastic classification of them all. Different state laws, and the federal bankruptcy laws where applicable, will protect different classes of these goods in different ways. What can be protected and up to what limit varies greatly state by state. To gain a rough idea of what you may be able to protect you should refer first to the appendix on exemptions.

But be aware this will only give you a rough idea. Each locale has different twists and nuances. One area may not treat golf clubs or fishing equipment as household goods. Pistols and rifles may or may not be treated as household goods. A pistol for home protection may be a household item, but a rifle that is used for hunting may not be. Iowa, for example, traditionally allows you to keep a rifle or shotgun.

Items may move from one category to another depending on how they are used. Art work hung on the wall can be a household item, but several drawings stacked up in a storage area may be classified as investment property rather than a household item. Your best guide is a lawyer who is aware of the local treatment of different items.

The lawyer will also be your best guide to evaluation. People's natural tendency is to value property at replacement value, or to give the price they paid for the item. But, the court system may allow you to value the items at yard sale value or some other value that is significantly below what you paid for it.

Often the court system will not push too hard on items such as furniture, appliances, and clothing. These are relatively low value items and as a practical matter the trustee would lose money if he or she tried to take them and sell them to raise funds to pay creditors. Time would cost more than the relatively small amounts the items would bring at an auction.

The story is quite different for other items with a ready identifiable market and resale value. Jewelry, silver, baseball cards, and other collections may have high value and be relatively easy for the trustee to sell.

Tools

Tools can generally be divided into two types: those used for hobby purposes and those used for business or work (tools of the trade). Hobby tools would have to be protected under household goods, if they could be protected at all.

Tools of trade are items you use to make a living and they are what is most likely to apply to you as a business operator. These can vary. New Hampshire allows you one yoke of oxen used for teaming; Nevada allows a cabin for mining and a mining claim; and, the District of Columbia protects the seal and documents of a Notary Public. Almost all have a "catch-all" rule for tools and books. Once again valuation is very important. Most people's first instinct is to value at what they paid for the tools. The better course is to value at what they would bring if you sold them in a short period of time— say two or three weeks.

In some states the level of protection can be depressingly low. This often presents a hard choice to the person contemplating a bankruptcy filing. If you will lose your tools or books if you file a Chapter 7 bankruptcy, you are out of business and cannot earn a livelihood. A lawyer is not much good without his or her law books and computers, and a mechanic without his or her wrenches. It is the need to keep the tools and equipment that causes many small business people to consider a Chapter 13 bankruptcy, even if they qualify for Chapter 7.

Other items of personal property

There is a vast number of items that do not fall into the categories of vehicles, household goods, and business tools. Depending on the state, these may or may not be protected. Examples of items that are protected are: church pews (Delaware), articles of adornment (Colorado), athletic and sporting equipment (Texas), and required arms and uniforms (Nevada).

Generally items such as tanning beds, boats, campers, etc, will be hard to keep, but the levels of protected goods are so varied from state to state, that you should always check with a lawyer before making your plans.

Retirement savings

You may have carefully saved money for retirement over the years. Generally, as long as the retirement program (company pension plan, IRA, 401(K), etc) is *ERISA* qualified, it will be protected. (ERISA is a federal law that regulates retirement plans.) Most pension programs are so protected. Occasionally small business people make mistakes in how they manage the retirement money and move outside the protected zone. So for example, if you are the trustee of your company retirement program, do not give the money to your brother-in-law to invest in a trailer park, or to operate a rabbit ranch.

Leased equipment

This is often a major category for the small businessperson. Often the business depends on leased equipment to operate. These can range from restaurants to dentist offices. The right to use the equipment is a property right, but it is useless if you cannot make the payments. The bankruptcy trustee is normally not all that interested in taking leased equipment as he cannot sell it (it belongs to the lessor). This often allows the business owner a choice to keep the business going. If the business can keep operating and generating enough funds to pay the lease payments then the business has a chance of surviving.

Accounts receivable

Often businesses or businessmen have accounts receivable, which they have not been able to collect or which are simply outstanding. One of the factors that brings on financial problems for small businesspeople is not being able to collect on accounts receivable. In taking your financial inventory, you should classify these accounts into likely collectible, possible, and bad debts. If you should have to file bankruptcy, the trustee will want an assessment of how likely it is that a given accounts receivable can be collected.

Section 12
What Will I Lose?

There is a widespread belief that you will lose all your property if you file bankruptcy. This is often not the case. There are ways to predict what you might you lose and how to make an assessment of what is at risk.

What is protected in bankruptcy and what is lost will depend in large part on what state you live in. Appendix B gives a state-by-state breakdown of levels of protection in the different states.

In looking to see what will be lost in bankruptcy, it should be remembered that after you file, two sets of people have an interest in your property. First there is the *trustee* whose duty is to collect property that is not exempt and sell it for the benefit of your creditors. The state exemptions set out what is *exempt* or protected from the trustee taking property.

The second group is the *secured creditors*. These are entities such as mortgage holders on your home or lien holders on your cars and trucks. If they are not paid they can repossess your home or vehicle. Often a trustee will not be interested in property because more is owed on it than it is worth. This means the trustee would not make any money from the general creditors if the property were seized and sold. So the trustee does not bother with the property.

Let's take two small business people, Sue and Tom, and see how they would be treated in three different states: North Carolina, Texas, and Delaware.

SUE:

Sue has been careful in starting her business and has limited what she has bought over the years. She has one child, age 10, who loves to ride horses. Her one luxury is a horse for the child to ride after school and on week-ends. Sue has debts of $70,000, which are a mix of business and personal debts, and has the following property.

	Equity
1) A home with a market value of $100,000. The first and second mortgages total $102,000.	$0 ($100,000 - $102,000)
2) An SUV worth $26,000. She owes $27,000 on it.	$0 (26,000 - 27,000)
3) A second vehicle worth $3,000.	$3,000
4) Tools and equipment used in her business worth $2,000.	$2,000
5) Household furnishings and clothes worth $4,000.	$4,000
6) A 401(k) with $50,000 in stock.	$50,000
7) A horse worth $1,500	$1,500

TOM:

Tom has spent more than Sue in running his business and owns property worth more than Sue. Tom also has one child, age 10, who loves to ride horses. His one luxury is a horse for the child to ride after school and on week-ends. Tom has debts of $140,000 and has the following property:

	Equity
1) A home with a market value of $200,000. The first and second mortgages on the home equal $45,000.	$165,000
2) An SUV worth $26,000. He owes $16,000 on it.	$10,000
3) A second vehicle worth $3,000.	$3,000
4) Tools and equipment worth $4,000, used in his business.	$4,000
5) Household furnishings and clothes worth $8,000.	$8,000
6) A 401(k) with $100,000 in stocks.	$100,000
7) A horse worth $3,000.	$3,000

How these two people are treated in a Chapter 7 bankruptcy will differ greatly in our three sample states. First, let us consider North Carolina.

NORTH CAROLINA:

The applicable property values that can be protected (not used for bankruptcy and left to the debtor) in North Carolina are as follows:

1) Home Equity $10,000

2) Car Equity (for 1 car) $1,500

3) Work Tools and Equipment $750

4) Household goods $3,500

5) Extra protection for household $750
   goods for each dependent

6) A "wild card" of up to $3,500 $3,500
   for the first $3,500 of house
   equity not used. (A "wild card" can be used to protect anything.)

In North Carolina Sue will have her property treated as follows:

1) Home   √ Can keep
   (There is $0 equity in the home so the Trustee
   will not take it to sell for the benefit of creditors.
   She will need to continue to pay the first and second mortgages to protect the home from the
   mortgage holders.)

2) SUV   √ Can keep
   (There is $0 equity in the SUV so the Trustee will
   not take it to sell for the benefit of creditors. She
   will need to continue to pay the lien holder to
   protect the SUV from the lien holders.)

3) Second vehicle   √ Protected
   (It is worth $3,000. The $1,500 vehicle protection can be applied against this. The other
   $1,500 can be protected by using $1,500 of the
   $3,500 wild card.)

4) Work tools and equipment   √ Protected
        (They are worth $2,000. The first $750 is pro-
        tected by the work tool exemption. The next
        $1,750 is protected by using $1750 of the $3500
        wild card.)

5) Household goods   √ Protected
        (They are worth $4,000. Sue can protect $3,500
        worth of household goods and her child $750.)

6) Stock in 401(k)   √ Protected
        (All money in a pension plan is protected by the
        Bankruptcy Code.)

7) Horse   ○ Not Fully Protected
        (Sue can use $750 of her remaining wild card to
        protect part of the value of the horse.)

TEXAS:

In Texas, the property values that can be protected are as follows:

1) Home equity   Unlimited
        (There is no limit on the value of homestead.
        There is a limit on the number of acres.)

2) Miscellaneous: $60,000
        (Can protect home furnishings, clothes, 1 motor
        vehicle, tools of trade and 2 horses as long as the
        total value is less than $60,000 for the head of a
        household.)

———————————————

In Texas Sue will have her property treated as follows:

1) Home   √ Can Keep
        (There is $0 equity in the home so the Trustee
        will not take it to sell for the benefit of creditors.
        She will need to continue to pay the first and sec-
        ond mortgages to protect the home from the
        mortgage holders.)

2) SUV   √ Can keep

> (There is $0 equity in the SUV so the Trustee will not take it to sell for the benefit of creditors. She will need to continue to pay the lien holder to protect the SUV from the lien holders.)

3) Second vehicle   √ Protected

> (Sue would use her one car protection for this vehicle as part of her general $60,000 exemption.)

4) Work tools and Equipment   √ Protected

> (Part of her $60,000 exemption)

5) Household goods   √ Protected

> (Part of her $60,000 exemption)

6) Stock in 401(k)   √ Protected

> (All money in a pension plan is protected by the Bankruptcy Code.)

7) Horse   √ Protected

> (Part of her $60,000 exemption)

DELAWARE:

In Delaware, the applicable property values that can be protected are as follows:

1) Homestead   * (see below)

2) Vehicle   * (see below)

3) Work tools and equipment   up to $75
   depending on the county

4) Household goods   * (see below)

> * A person has a general $5,000 exemption which can be used to protect the filer's property. In certain instances exemption may be applied to protect homestead exemption.

The result for Sue in Delaware is as follows:

1) Home   √ Can keep

(There is $0 equity in the home so the Trustee
will not take it to sell for the benefit of creditors.
She will need to continue to pay the first and second mortgages to protect the home from the
mortgage holders.)

2) SUV   √ Can keep

(There is $0 equity in the SUV so the Trustee will
not take it to sell for the benefit of creditors. She
will need to continue to pay the lien holder to
protect the SUV from the lien holders.)

3) Second vehicle   ○ Part can be protected
(see below)

4) Work tools and equipment   ○ Part can be protected
(see below)
(Can at best protect only $75 in
work tools)

5) Household goods   ○ Part can be protected
(see below)

6) Stock in 401(k)   √ Protected

(All money in a pension plan is protected by the
Bankruptcy Code.)

7) Horse   ○ Part of value can be protected
(see below)
Sue will need to choose how to allocate her
$5,000 exemption among her different groups of
property. She elected to use her $5,000 to protect
all her household goods ($4,000) and part of her
work tools ($1,000).

TOM:

How would Tom be treated in the different states? Tom owes more money and has property of a higher value than Sue. To recap Tom's property:

	Equity
1) A home with a market value of $200,000. The first and second mortgages on the home equal $45,000.	$165,000
2) An SUV worth $26,000. He owes $16,000 on it.	$10,000
3) A second vehicle worth $3,000.	$3,000
4) Tools and equipment worth $4,000, used in his business.	$4,000
5) Household furnishings and clothes worth $8,000.	$8,000
6) A 401(k) with $100,000 in stocks.	$100,000
4) A horse worth $3,000.	$3,000

The results for Tom would be as follows:

In North Carolina:

1) House   ○ Not protected
(The $165,000 in equity is far larger than the $10,000 protected zone.)

2) SUV   ○ Not protected
(The $10,000 in equity is far larger than the $1500 vehicle protected zone.)

3) Second vehicle   √ Protected
(It is worth $3,000. The $1,500 vehicle protection can be applied against this. Since the house is lost, the other $1,500 can be protected using $1,500 of the $3,500 wild card gained when the house was lost.)

4) Work tools and equipment   √ Protected
    (They are worth $2,000. The first $750 is pro-
    tected by the work tool exemption and the next
    $1,750 by the wild card exemption gained from
    the wild card.)

5) Household goods   √ Protected
    (They are worth $4,000. Tom can protect $3,500
    worth of household goods and his child $750.)

6) Stock in 401(k)   √ Protected
    (All money in a pension plan is protected by the
    Bankruptcy Code.)

7) Horse   ◦ Not fully protected
    (Tom can use $750 of his remaining wild card to
    protect part of the value of the horse.)

In Texas the result is:

1) Home   √ Protected
    (There is no dollar limit on home value—only an
    acre limit.)

2) SUV   √ Protected
    (Part of his $60,000 exemption)

3) Second vehicle   ◦ Not protected
    (He can only protect one vehicle.)

4) Work tools and equipment   √ Protected
    (Part of his $60,000 exemption)

5) Household goods   √ Protected
    (Part of his $60,000 exemption)

6) Stock in 401(k)   √ Protected
    (All money in a pension plan is protected by the
    Bankruptcy Code.)

7) Horse   √ Protected
    (Part of his $60,000 exemption)

In Delaware the result is the same for Tom as it was for Sue.

1) Home   ○ Not protected

2) SUV   ○ Not protected

3) Second vehicle   ○ Not protected

3) Work tools and equipment   ○ Up to $75
   depending on the county

5) Household goods   ○ Partly Protected
   Tom used all of his $5,000 exemption to protect
   as much of his household goods as possible.

6) Stock in 401(k)   √ Protected
   (All money in a pension plan is protected by the
   Bankruptcy Code.)

7) Horse   ○ Not protected
   A few observations are in order. The result did
   not depend on the size of the unsecured debt.
   But it did vary on the amount of secured debt
   against homes and vehicles. Clearly Texas is the
   best place to live if you have to file bankruptcy,
   and Delaware is the worst place to file.

Texas and Delaware are extreme examples. Most states fall somewhere in between. The states vary greatly in how they treat different items of property and in what dollar limits they place on each class of property. However, in most states you increase your likelihood of losing property if you have assets such as vehicles and homes that are almost paid off.

People who live in states with low zones of protection have the option of filing a Chapter 13 bankruptcy. They will have to pay out in the Chapter 13 at least what the creditors would have received in a Chapter 7, but they have several years to do so.

Section 13
Do's and Don'ts of Filing for Bankruptcy

Eventually even the most optimistic businessperson starts to realize that bankruptcy is a real possibility. When this happens people naturally begin to think of steps that they can take to protect their hard earned property for their families. Some of these steps will merely cause problems when and if bankruptcy is filed, while others may consist of fraud and cause the person to end up in jail.

Common steps people consider are:

- paying themselves bonuses after no pay;
- taking goods from business;
- paying off loans to family members and close friends;
- transferring or sell property to family or friends at a low price;
- paying off their car loans;
- buying a new car or a reliable car; or,
- hiding assets

Paying Themselves Bonuses after No Pay

When a business begins to have cash flow problems, most entrepreneurs will reduce their draws or stop paying themselves altogether. Then when it looks like the business may have to be bankrupted, they start thinking about the extra money in the corporate bank account, and how they have not been paid for their very hard work. There is a strong temptation to pay themselves a bonus or to pay off the loans to themselves they put on the company books when they did not draw a salary.

Do not do this. When the corporation goes into a Chapter 7 bankruptcy (a corporation cannot file a Chapter 13), the trustee is likely to view this as fraud and at the very least force you to pay the money back to the corporation. Remember, a corporation is a separate legal entity and you have a special relationship to it. You cannot use your power over the corporation as the proprietor in charge to take money out to pay one creditor (yourself) or to pay management (yourself). To do so runs the risk of adding to your money problems, the vastly greater problems of federal bankruptcy crimes. Every year people go to jail for bankruptcy fraud.

The problem is similar if you are not incorporated. If you are not incorporated the temptation to pay money to yourself out of the business bank account will be much smaller as the business creditors will also be your personal creditors. So all you are doing is moving money from one pocket to another. The creditors can still get to the money whether it is in your personal bank account or in the business bank account.

Taking Goods from Business

Closely allied with taking money out of the business is the practice of taking tools and equipment from a business that is about to go under. This is a special temptation when you have small mobile items such as Palm Pilots or portable computers. These items are not titled, will have little liquidation value to the business, and may be expensive to buy if you have to buy them new. Software falls into the same category. People tend to see such takings as little white thefts, if they think of it as a theft at all. But again, to remove items that the corporation paid for prior to bankruptcy is bankruptcy fraud and is really not worth it.

Paying off Loans to Family Members and to Close Friends

Payments to family are specifically forbidden by the bankruptcy code. In fact, any payment to insiders, such as family, within a one year period can be recaptured by the trustee. This is clearly true if you make a last minute repayment of loans to the business as a lump sum.

But, this can trap you when you have a practice of making monthly payments to your family members for a loan they made to you. Let's say you borrowed $10,000 from your folks a year ago. Since then you have paid $500 back to them each month as a loan repayment (a total of $6,000 has been paid to them). The trustee can go to your parents and make them give the $6,000 back to the trustee to be paid out to other creditors.

The terrible part of this trap is that often parents have borrowed against their houses or their retirement accounts to make the loan. They do not have the $6,000 to pay back, and if the child can't pay them back they risk losing their home or a large part of their retirement.

Since repayments to parents have such negative consequences you should never borrow money from family members, when it is money they cannot afford to simply write off. Borrowing from your family to fund the start-up of your business, or when the business hits a down turn seems like a good idea. They will lend to you when often no one else will. But, it is a terrible trap if they can't afford to write off any money they lent to you.

Transferring or Selling Property to Family or Friends at a "Sweetheart Price"

A closely allied temptation when considering bankruptcy is to sell or transfer goods to family members. When people begin to realize the limited scope of property that can be protected, their first thought is to simply "get it out of their name." This is often done with noble interest. For example, a child's car may have been put in his or her parent's name for insurance purposes, or because the child could not qualify for the loan when it was purchased. Everyone knows it was the child's car, because he or she paid for it, but somehow it was never put in his or her name. When the parents file bankruptcy since the car title is in the parent's name, it is considered their property and subject to being taken by the bankruptcy court. Often debtors feel it is unfair that the child will lose his or her car because of a legal technicality. Thus people want to transfer the car title to the child where it "really should be."

Bankruptcy is a maze of technicalities and steps to "fix" the legalities. The facts as you and the family understand them can rapidly lead to large problems in bankruptcy. The sale of property for too low a price to a family member or a friend or simply giving it to them can lead both you and the other party into real trouble. The bankruptcy forms ask about such transactions and you will be faced with the decision to tell about them or to lie.

To tell the truth will cause the transaction to be undone, and likely cause heightened review of your whole case by the trustee. If you lie, it is bankruptcy fraud and the exposure to a criminal conviction of a federal crime. It is far better to work your way through the bankruptcy with the facts as you have them when you started having money problems.

Paying Off Car Loans

Cars and what to do about them are also a fruitful source of missteps for people who are having money problems. Many people after a little research or after asking around come to the understanding that the bankruptcy laws allow them to keep a car. So they pay off their car shortly before seeing a lawyer, or they may have made a point of making their car payments right along and now own their car free and clear.

This is as bad as having too much equity in a house. Take a look at your state's exemption for a motor vehicle. You will be shocked. Most exemptions are in the $1,000–$3,000 range, and often you are not allowed to use wholesale values (You are often allowed to use a value between wholesale and retail, just where depends on your district). If the car has a value above your state exemption then you must either give the car up (and receive back money equal to the state exemption where it is sold), or pay the difference, assuming you can raise from family the money to pay the difference. You are in effect paying for the vehicle twice. Once when you paid for it, and a second time to the trustee to keep it.

It is far better to owe money on your car as this will reduce the value of the car. Say you have a vehicle worth $10,000. If you own it free and clear you would have to pay an amount equal to $10,000 less your state exemption. However if you owed $9,000 on the car you would only have a value of $1,000. That is probably within your state's protected zone for vehicles, and you would need to pay nothing to the trustee. (Of course you would still need to pay the vehicle's lien holder or they could take the vehicle.)

Buying a New Car or a Reliable Car

The mirror image of having a fairly new car which is paid for can present a trap in bankruptcy. When people have an old, unreliable car as they start to have money problems and to consider bankruptcy, they may realize that the car is not likely to last the several years that a Chapter 13 will take, or that they will have a hard time finding someone to sell them a more reliable vehicle once they have filed bankruptcy. They may even have a little money on hand which they want to transform into something that can be protected in bankruptcy.

There are several potential traps in bankruptcy for this type of action. First, if the money is used to outright pay for all or a great deal of the vehicle, you are back in the trap covered in Section 9. The second is that often the exemptions will not be available if you filed too close to when you purchased the vehicle. And the seller may claim fraud if the purchase and the filing come too close together. Always check with a lawyer before you take this step. And if you are in the process of filling out the paper work for a bankruptcy, be doubly sure to talk to your bankruptcy lawyer about this. It is amazing how many people will buy cars while in the process of having the bankruptcy papers drawn up and never think to talk to the lawyer about it.

Hiding Assets

The most dangerous course of action when bankruptcy is near or is being filed is to hide assets. This can range from giving gold pins to a family member to hold, to not listing land owned in another state or county. As with taxes, this type of fraud is hard to spot so the government has made the punishment very harsh when they do pick up on it. Often people who do this type of thing are sent to jail.

How does the government find out about it? Ex-spouses, ex-friends and co-workers. It is amazing how much secretaries know. Creditors have lists of all the things you said you owned when you were trying to get your loan and do not look kindly on your trying to stiff them by hiding these assets in bankruptcy.

PART II
Types of Bankruptcy

Section 14
Chapter 7 Bankruptcy

Under the current law there are few restraints to filing a Chapter 7 bankruptcy and the process is fairly straightforward. As in filing your taxes, the great bulk of the work in a Chapter 7 is in collecting and classifying the information. Once the information is collected, it is recorded in the petition's ten schedules, the statement of Financial Affairs and the Statement of Intention.

The schedules are:

Schedule A	Real property
Schedule B	Personal property
Schedule C	Property claimed as exempt
Schedule D	Creditors holding secured claims
Schedule E	Creditors holding unsecured priority claims
Schedule F	Creditors holding unsecured nonpriority claims
Schedule G	Executory contracts and unexpired leases
Schedule H	Co-debtors
Schedule I	Current income
Schedule J	Current expenditures

The Automatic Stay

For many people one of the main reasons they file bankruptcy is to stop phone calls from creditors. The *automatic stay* is what accomplishes this.

The automatic stay is a court order forbidding contact with the debtor/petitioner by the creditor. The creditors are ordered to stop collection phone calls, letters and lawsuits. Because of the damages of legal action against them, most creditors stop all contacts with the debtor. This can be a problem for people who plan to keep on paying on a given debt and depend on the creditor sending them a coupon or reminder each month. Normally, even these will stop and often people get into trouble with the creditor for not making monthly payments on items they wish to keep.

If a creditor wants to continue to try and foreclose on your home, he or she must go to court and ask the judge to lift the stay. This is often granted in a Chapter 7 case. In a Chapter 13 case it is much harder for a creditor to have the automatic stay lifted.

Trustee

Once your petition is filed, it is given to a trustee for your case. The trustee's job is to represent the creditors in general and obtain as much money as he can from you. Your lawyer will use the exemptions your state provides to protect as much of your property and assets as possible.

Most of the trustee's review of your case is done in the trustee's office. In the typical case, your only contact with the trustee will be at the Section 341 meeting which takes place about a month after you file. There the trustee will ask you a short series of questions with two purposes in mind. The first is designed to get you on oath that you put a proper value on all listed property, that you listed all your property, and that you have not improperly transferred money or property to a third person. The second purpose is to ask questions about how you came up with the listed value for your home, car and other property.

Section 341 Meeting

The Section 341 meeting is often called a *meeting of creditors* or a *first meeting of creditors* as this is the creditor's chance to ask questions. The ringmaster of the meeting of creditors is the bankruptcy trustee. He or she is picked, normally on a rotating basis, from a panel of trustees for the court district. The trustees are normally experienced bankruptcy lawyers. They are not paid much for handling the case and normally they are undertaking to handle a great many routine, low-paying cases for the opportunity to work on a case that has enough assets to generate fees for the trustee. The trustee is liable for oversight to be sure he or she does a complete and timely job.

Reviewing the Petition

Before you are questioned at the meeting of creditors, the trustee's office will have reviewed your petition to be sure that a fair value has been placed on listed assets, for assets that have a value in excess of the protected zone provided in their state and in recent financial dealings. The latter include payments to creditors, (especially family members), just before the filing of the Chapter 7 petition, and the giving or selling of property close to the filing. If a trustee finds you have improperly transferred property to a creditor or family member, he or she can force the recipient to return the property.

Two situations often develop. A parent has title, often for insurance purposes, for a car that is really the child's. The parent transfers the title to the child just before filing to get the legal car title in alignment with the "true facts". Another common situation is that a person has borrowed money from a parent and each month makes a payment towards repaying the loan. In both of these cases, the trustee can force the recipient of the property or the money to *disgorge* (give up) what they have received. The value received is used to pay a fee to the trustee and to be divided among other creditors.

The trustee does not normally get involved with property you choose to surrender to a creditor. He or she will merely tell you or your lawyer to make arrangements with the creditor to deliver the property, or make it available for pickup, if you have not already done so.

Creditor Attendance

Normally, most creditors will not bother to come and ask questions. However, sometimes creditors do attend and have questions. They may ask about statements about assets and income you made on a loan application. This can be very embarrassing and troublesome if the statements on the loan application are different from what was listed in your bankruptcy petition. One occasionally sees creditors call attention to business equipment or other assets not listed on the bankruptcy petition.

The questions asked by the trustee and creditors are normally low-keyed. People's fears of being cross-examined, the way they see trials in lawyer-based dramas on T.V., do not come to pass. To start with, the format of doing many cases in a short period of time does not allow lengthy questions. Second, there is normally not much need for extended questioning as the information on the petition is accurate and complete. And the careful loan applicant will have put a fair value on all filed property in the loan application.

The atmosphere is much more casual than a trial. There is no judge present. Normally the trustee, the petitioner and his lawyer sit fairly close to each other. There are not all the many extra court officials one sees in a typical trial.

Others at the Meeting

People always ask if there will be other people at the meeting, as they fear having their personal affairs put on public display. There will be other people at the meeting, but almost all of them will be other people who have filed bankruptcy, lawyers, and a few representatives of creditors. We have never seen members of the general public at a meeting of creditors the way you sometimes see at a state court trial. The meetings of creditors are too boring and out of the way to attract bystanders.

After the 341 Meeting

In the vast majority of Chapter 7 cases, the hearing marks the last step in the process that involves the petitioner. The petitioner then waits about three months to receive his discharge letter.

There may be some ministerial steps. The filer may elect to reaffirm some debts. The normal reason to do this is to keep property, such as cars, on which the creditor has a lien and which the creditor could take. You should get the advice of your lawyer before signing such documents as in some areas a reaffirmation agreement is not necessary to retain property if the debt is current.

Following the meeting of creditors there is a short period of suspense, while you wait to see if any of your creditors will challenge you or otherwise cause problems. They have sixty days from the date of the first scheduled meeting of creditors in which to challenge the discharge of their debt. The sixty day date is called the bar date, as it bars creditors from raising objections after that date.

If nothing untoward happens, you should receive your discharge papers about three to five months after you filed your petition. (The difference in time will depend on how fast the court system can do its paperwork.) This letter normally states that you have received a bankruptcy discharge. It does not state which debts are discharged. For this reason, it is important to hold on to both your copy of the bankruptcy petition (which listed your creditors) and the discharge letter. They are the two halves of the whole. One shows what debts were listed and the other says that the listed debts are discharged.

Problems That Can Arise

In the great majority of cases, the meeting of creditors goes smoothly and all the petitioner need do is wait for his or her discharge papers. But sometimes problems do come up.

Transfers to Family

One has already been mentioned: transfers to family members within a year prior to the petition being filed. Another is large payments to one creditor within a short time of filing the petition. The system does not want one creditor to be favored over another. Thus if you made, say, a $1,000 payment to credit card X for one reason or another and paid nothing to the others, the trustee may force credit card X to disgorge the money.

Tax Refund

Depending on when the petition is filed, the petitioner may be entitled to or receive a tax refund within six months of the filing of the petition. It is always a surprise to people to learn that the trustee and the creditors are entitled to this money if it cannot be protected using the exemptions available in the applicable state.

Inheritances

Inheritances are another possible problem. If people are surprised to learn that the trustee has a potential claim on tax refunds, they are shocked and dismayed to learn that the trustee can take inheritances that accrue within six months of filing. In addition to the loss of a loved one, the person is faced with the loss of property which the family member spent a lifetime acquiring. This is a disaster as the protecting exemptions allowed by state and federal law typically do not come close to protecting what has been inherited. If an inheritance occurs the trustee will take enough of the petitioner's share of the estate to pay all filed claims and pay for his or her time. Occasionally the inherited money is sufficiently large to allow for a return of some of the money to the filer after all filed claims and administrative expenses have been paid, but this does not happen often.

Logically the petitioner is not much worse off than he or she would have been if he or she had inherited the money the week before filing the bankruptcy petition. In such a case, he or she would have paid off the debts and have kept what was left. And he or she may be better off, for often his or her share of the inheritance is not large enough to pay off the debts. But, people often do not see it that way. They tend to mentally divide the money into different pots. This pot is the debts and it has to get along on its own. The other pot is the family inheritance and it is viewed as a one-time thing, and is his or hers only. Often people think about the improvements they could make to their homes, education payments for children, or dream vacations. Thus it is very painful to lose the money that would have paid for these things.

Forgetting to List Something

Sometimes in the stress and rush of preparing the bankruptcy petition, a person will find that they forgot to list a debt or an asset. This can easily be overcome, if it is discovered shortly after filing the petition, by doing an amendment to the petition. If it is found later it can be a larger problem. The trustee or a creditor may conclude you were trying to hide the asset. And if the case has been closed without a creditor being listed you may not have that debt discharged. Normally only creditors listed in the bankruptcy have their debts done away with. Even in such a case there may be ways around this, but it is far better and safer to be very thorough when you supply information for the court in the original filing.

Other Problems

Other problems can come up from strict policies of creditors. Sometimes hospitals will refuse to release medical information because their debt was discharged in a bankruptcy. Other times creditors, or someone who purchased the debt, will try to collect on a debt that was listed and discharged in bankruptcy. Lenders may refuse to grant a loan until you prove that a given debt was discharged in your bankruptcy. (This often occurs because the credit report is not complete or correct.) Most of these problems can be overcome by being careful to hold on to your discharge letter and petition.

Section 15

Chapter 11 and
Chapter 13 Bankruptcy

This section will examine how Chapters 11 and 13 bankruptcies proceed. They are different from Chapter 7 bankruptcies discussed in Section 14.

Chapter 11

The goal of a Chapter 11 bankruptcy filing is to stop the business's destructive spiral. It gives everyone time to collect facts to see if the company, perhaps on a greatly stripped-down level, can continue to operate, or whether it should be *liquidated* (all assets sold) in an orderly manner.

In a business the concern often has a great deal more value than the sum of its assets. Often business equipment brings very little when sold. This is because the assets of most businesses are so specialized that they cannot be used for other purposes by other businesses. In addition, of course, the *good will* and *trade name* are lost if the business is shut down. Society and the stake holders in the business—employees, customers, creditors, and even owners—will achieve the best value if the business can be kept alive.

Sometimes a Chapter 11 is used to avoid unwise contracts that have become an unbearable drag on the company's chance for profitability. This may be a vendor contract or leases.

In other cases there is a desire to sell the business assets or operation as an ongoing business. The Chapter 11 can give you time to dispose of the business in an orderly way. The filing prevents one or two creditors from destroying the business by seizing key property or assets.

Legal Steps

There are several distinct legal steps in a Chapter 11 proceeding. First, just like any other bankruptcy, a petition must be filed. This brings the individual or corporation under the protection of the bankruptcy system. Normally the owners or management will want to continue to run the business as "debtor possession." The court has the final say over whether or not this will be allowed, but normally the interests of everyone are served by having the people who best know the business continue to operate it.

However, because the business and its property have come under the *jurisdiction* of the court, reports are typically required to give a running account of what is being done by the debtor in possession and in particular how assets are being disposed of. This often means filing a monthly report with the court and this can be a hard burden on an overworked small businessperson. A large company would simply have an accountant (requiring court approval). A struggling small business may not be able to afford to have a third party do this report.

Committee of Creditors

The creditors cannot be disregarded after the filing. The U.S. Bankruptcy Code provides for the creation of one or more committees of creditors. These are small groups that represent the creditors in general. This small group is often a big help to businesses who have thousands of creditors to deal with, but may not be much help to a small business that has only a few creditors to begin with.

There is a meeting of creditors where the debtor has the opportunity to explain his or her situation to creditors—what went wrong, and how the future of the business can be protected. The creditors have the chance to ask questions of the petitioner or his or her representative.

Independent Reports

Often an independent party is appointed to study the business and give an independent report on its problems and prospects. The petitioner is typically expected to pay the fees of this independent party.

Disclosure Statement

A *disclosure statement* must be prepared, which after approval by the court will be sent to creditors as part of the next legal step—solicitations for acceptance of the plan of reorganization. The disclosure statement gives a summary of the plan of reorganization and how the different types of creditors will be treated. A general overview of the finances of the filing entity are to be given and what would happen if other alternatives, such as complete liquidation, were followed.

The statement would also alert the reader to risk factors involved in the different alternatives facing the business or person. A hearing on the disclosure statement is held before it and the plan of reorganization can be sent to interested parties. Since the disclosure statement summarizes the plan of reorganization, the plan of reorganization must be thought out early in the process.

Plan of Reorganization

The heart of the Chapter 11 is the *plan of reorganization*. It spells out how each different class of creditor is to be treated. A *class* is one or more creditors who share similar situations. Part of the art of doing a Chapter 11 is knowing how the different creditors can be put in one or more classes as the needs of the situation require. How creditors are classed is very important as a vote of creditors on the plan will be taken and approval of different classes must be obtained.

The ideal is the approval of every class that is *impaired,* or is receiving less than what is owed them. This of course may not happen and in that case the court can *cram down* their interest—make them take less if some technical rules are followed. Since a vote of a majority of the members of a given class is required for approval by that class, the make-up of the different classes is very important.

It is a mistake to blindly put together a plan for reorganization and put it to a vote without having a pretty good idea of how key classes will vote. In this way if you see a group of creditors that does not like a provision you have the chance to change your proposal before it is written up and mailed out.

Normally, in addition to asking what the creditors think, the debtor and his or her lawyer will negotiate with the creditors about the treatment of their class. Often the creditor must be educated as to what the alternatives are. No creditor likes receiving less than what was contracted for, so the creditor must be made to see that accepting the proposal with its economic loss is better than any of the alternatives.

Often this disintegrates into a game where the creditor has the option to try to "kill" the reorganization by voting against the plan. They use this power to try to force better terms. The debtor wants the business to keep on operating; that is why he or she filed a Chapter 11. But, the plan must leave the debtor a reasonable chance to succeed. Agreeing to an unrealistic plan provision that will surely kill the plan does not help anyone at all.

Chapter 13 Bankruptcy

A Chapter 13 bankruptcy as filed is a hybrid between a Chapter 7 and a Chapter 11. The typical Chapter 13 filer has one or more of three motivations. An important reason for many people is that the creditors will receive back some of the money they loaned you. "I made these debts and I have always paid my debts" is a common statement. People are willing to put up with the problems inherent in the Chapter 13 process out of the moral or psychological wish to pay at least some of their debts back.

Another reason people file Chapter 13 is to save their homes or cars. Unlike Chapter 7, a Chapter 13 is designed to stop foreclosures and repossessions. The creditor can object if the proposed Chapter 13 repayment plan is unrealistic or if the property will depreciate faster than the creditor is paid under the plan. However, given a reasonable plan, a Chapter 13 program will allow a debtor a chance to save his or her home and car and make up missed payments a little each month.

This latter factor is very important in dealing with homes. Many Chapter 13 filers are people who, for one reason or another, missed monthly house payments. Often the creditor's response is to demand that all back payments be made as a lump sum and they refuse to take offered monthly payments. If a person can't pay all back payments at once, his only option may be to file a Chapter 13. The other options, refinancing their home and debt consolidation loans, typically are not available because of the black mark on their credit caused by the missed house payments.

A third reason people file Chapter 13 is it affords them the chance to retain property they would lose in a Chapter 7. Chapter 7 filers have the possibility of losing property, especially business property, no matter which of the three sample states they lived in. This is a common occurrence in every state. This is a problem for business people as state exemptions tend to concentrate on pocketing people's homes and personal household-related items.

Much of this personal and business property can be protected in Chapter 13. As long as creditors receive at least what they would have received in Chapter 7, the Chapter 13 will work. The amount the creditors receive does not need to be paid all at once as would be the case in Chapter 7. The payment can be stretched out over the three to five year life of the Chapter 13.

Operation of a Chapter 13

The structure of a Chapter 13 petition is similar to a Chapter 7 petition. It has ten schedules. In addition, it has a proposed plan, which sets out how debts are to be paid. There is also a statement of financial affairs. The schedules are:

Schedule A	Real property
Schedule B	Personal property
Schedule C	Property claused as exempt
Schedule D	Secured creditors
Schedule E	Priority creditors
Schedule F	Unsecured creditors

Schedule G	Executory contracts and unexpired leases
Schedule H	Co-debtors
Schedule F	Current income
Schedule F	Current expenses

Proposed Plan

The heart of the Chapter 13 is the plan, which sets out how each class of creditors will be paid. It is similar to a Chapter 11 plan, but less complex, as it is dealing with a wage earning individual or an individual who operates a small business rather than a large, complex business.

It will set out how long the plan will last—three to five years—and what will be paid to the trustee and to the lawyer who represented the debtor.

It will then list how the different main classes of creditors will be paid. Secured creditors may either be paid in full or partially paid in full and partially paid as unsecured creditors. Debtors may choose to pay co-signed claims in full to protect the co-signers.

The plan will state how back taxes and student loans will be treated. It will also set out how fast arrearages will be repaid. The plan will also state in a general way how the unsecured claims—credit cards, personal loans, medical bills, etc.—will be treated. This is the "plug" number in most plans as there is often a general understanding in a given area about what percentage must be paid to unsecured general creditors. If the proposed plan is too aggressive in limiting what is paid to creditors they can object and a court hearing will be held.

Two *overarching* constraints limit the plan. First, the unsecured creditors must receive at least what they would have received in a Chapter 7 bankruptcy. Second, the debtor must devote all or substantially all of his or her *disposable income* to the repayment plan. Disposable income is money available from income after reasonable living expenses. This opens another avenue for disputes as a creditor or trustee may have an objection stating that a given debtor's living expenses are not reasonable.

Areas of dispute in addition to the normal cost of food and entertainment issues are expenses for charitable giving, repayment of loans against retirement plans, and the cost of private schooling for the debtor's children. The plan will also state what creditors are to be paid directly, what property is to be surrendered, and what executory contracts and leases will be kept or given up.

After the Plan is Filed

A first meeting of creditors is held where creditors can question the debtor, and then there is time allowed for the creditors to object to the plan. At the time of filing the creditors are notified to file their claims with the court stating how much they believe they are owed. It is not uncommon for this amount to be different from what the debtor claims he or she owes. The debtor can object to the claim if he or she thinks it is incorrect. A hearing would then be held to see which party is correct.

If there are no objections by either party, the plan goes into effect as written and is binding on all parties.

Post Plan Problems

A Chapter 13 plan lasts for three to five years and during that time the debtor has a special relationship with the court. In a Chapter 7 filing, the trustee takes what property he or she can and sells it. In a Chapter 13 the debtor is allowed to keep and use the property but is accountable to the court for its use. He or she is treated as a *debtor in possession of bankruptcy property,* or debtor in possession. Since the court could have taken the property to settle debts, but did not, the debtor must stand ready to account for this property.

Sale of Property

The main time this debtor-in-possession theory causes a problem is when people want to sell their home or their vehicles. Since it is the property of the bankruptcy estate a people are not free to just sell the property and pocket the money. They must first obtain permission of the court for the sale and account for the money received. By the same token you cannot, for example, just give a vehicle to your child because everyone in the family knows it is really the child's car.

New Debt

While you are under Chapter 13 you are not allowed to incur more debt. This means you must stop charging on credit cards and cannot borrow money during the life of the plan without the court's or trustee's specific permission. This often causes problems when cars wear out or when the debtor must move.

Before the court will allow new or additional debt they will want to know the terms of the new debt, what is being bought and why. Be sure the additional debt can be repaid without hurting the old creditors.

Car Wrecks

A problem that is fairly common during the life of the Chapter 13 plan is a car wreck. Sometimes it seems that car wrecks seek out people in Chapter 13's. In a certain number of these wrecks the debtor's car will be totalled. This means the debtor must replace the car and will need new financing. The system allows for this financing to be done by the old lien holder, if there is one, with the old lien holder obtaining a lien on the new car.

In practice this can be a problem. If a car is totalled by the insurance company it often does not pay enough to replace the car. The creditor, if it is to substitute collateral, will want a car at least as valuable as the one that was wrecked and does not care that the insurance pay off was not enough to purchase such a car. Often the creditor will refuse to allow any substitution on collateral and the debtor must ask for help from the court. All of this takes time, and the debtor may very well have to pay extra money to obtain the replacement car. This is very hard on debtors who are without a car to drive to work and short of ready cash.

Insurance Lapses

When a person takes out a loan on a car, a standard clause in his or her loan agreement requires him or her to keep *collision insurance*. This will allow the lender to recover some of the loaned money if something happens to the car.

Once in a Chapter 13, people often have a hard time making ends meet. They may have suffered a drop in income or have agreed to a repayment plan they really could not quite afford in an effort to save a home or a car. To make ends meet there is a temptation to let insurance premium payments slide.

This is a mistake. The creditor has the ability to repossess cars when the debtor fails to keep insurance on the car, as required by the security agreement. The idea behind this is that the creditor is being kept by the bankruptcy filing from taking the car, and in exchange the debtor has a duty to give the creditor the protection offered by the collision insurance policy.

Drop in Income

A common question when people are considering a Chapter 13 is, "What happens if I have a drop in my income or unexpected expenses?" This is a real problem for self-employed businesspeople as their income from month to month is not steady. They often have slow sales during certain seasons.

The short answer is that you are expected to make the Chapter 13 monthly payment whether or not you have a shortfall in a given month because of decreased income or higher expenses. Sometimes the trustee will give you a chance to make up a short payment. However, this is often not much help. What is often done is that you will be expected to make increased payments until the shortfall is made up in a short period of time. Often people find themselves in a sort of downward spiral. They could not pay their payment of X and now they must pay X plus an amount to make up the missed payment. Unless the shortfall was a one-time blip this may be impossible and they will be dropped from the Chapter 13 program.

Section 16
Post Filing Issues

With a few exceptions, the filing of bankruptcy sets your financial picture. It is like a financial snapshot was taken on the day you filed your bankruptcy petition. What you have in your possession is reachable by the bankruptcy trustee, and to protect it you must use the exemptions allowed by applicable state and federal law. However, there are exceptions to this general rule.

Inheritances

In a Chapter 7 proceeding, money you inherit within six months after you file your petition is subject to being taken by the trustee for benefit of creditors. This is always a terrible shock to people in addition to the sadness of the loss of a loved one—normally a parent. The filer stands to lose much of what his or her family member worked so hard to build up. The general rules of *exemptions* apply to inheritances, but usually inheritances are so large that the exemption protection does not help much.

In a Chapter 13, having an inheritance runs into two problems. The first is the general rule that creditors in a Chapter 13 should receive at least what creditors in a Chapter 7 would have received. The second is the *disposable income test*. People in a Chapter 13 are supposed to devote all of their disposable income to the Chapter 13 plan. If you inherit money you have more to pay your creditors with.

Tax Refunds

The same general rules apply to tax refunds above your protected limit. Here the *wild card*, exemptions in any asset allowed if you did not use your homestead exemption, may be useful. A $2,000 protection zone may not be very helpful in the case of an inheritance, but could be enough to protect a major portion of a tax refund. In a multi-year Chapter 13 plan, tax refunds do not normally come into consideration.

Gifts from the Family or Friends

Money you receive as a gift from your family after filing a bankruptcy is normally protected. This means that a family member or a friend could purchase a car or other items for you. In many cases such people buy items and property from the trustee as part of the sale of assets procedure.

This is particularly helpful to businesspeople who want to keep their business going but who need to purchase phone numbers or other assets of the business to achieve this goal.

Deceiving the Trustee

The trustee learning about your inheritance or a tax refund depends to a great extent on the honor system. There is not a central repository that lists inheritances or tax refunds. The trustee may never know about the inheritance or tax refund if you do not tell him. This creates a strong incentive to cheat the system by never telling anyone about it.

Not revealing assets such as inheritance and tax refunds are bankruptcy crimes and people who hide assets are subject to federal criminal prosecution. You could go to jail. Do not expect your lawyer to help you hide these assets. Lawyers are forbidden to help people commit a crime.

Income Increases

In a Chapter 7 bankruptcy filing, most of the time good fortune that befalls you after you file bankruptcy is good fortune that does not need to be shared. If you land a new, higher-paying job or get a raise in your present job the increase is yours. The idea of the Chapter 7 bankruptcy is to give you a fresh start in life. If the creditors or the bankruptcy system could reach out and seize property as you are trying to rebuild your life, this purpose would be defeated.

A Chapter 13 proceeding can be different. In a Chapter 7 filing, a snap shot of one's financial affairs is taken the day you file and that is basically all there is to it. But, in a Chapter 13, you subject yourself and your property to the review of the court for several years. This gives time for the disposable income test to bite you.

Some Chapter 13 courts, trustees, and creditors will take the position that if you are earning more money you have more disposable income to pay to your creditors and may push for a larger payment to your creditors. Normally this is not a problem. As your income rises your reasonable living expenses will also increase. The net result is that no more disposable income is available for creditors.

But, this concept can be a problem for small business owners. It is not unheard of for a business, for whatever reason, to take off after a Chapter 13 is filed. Far more money is being generated for the businessperson than before the case was filed.

If more money is coming in, the trustee, court, or creditor may invoke the disposable income rule and call for much of this money to go to the Chapter 13 trustee to pay on debts. This will often come to the attention of the Chapter 13 trustee because many of them review monthly business reports from people in Chapter 13 who are operating a business.

The increase in income can come to the attention of the Chapter 13 trustee in the case of a businessperson or a regular wage earner in another way. It is not uncommon for a person in a Chapter 13 to need to buy another car or a new house during the three to five years the Chapter 13 plan lasts. To undertake new indebtedness to purchase a car or house requires the permission of the court or trustee. This permission will not be forthcoming unless the person can afford it.

People will then reveal their higher income in an effort to show they can afford the requested purchase. With this information in front of them, the court, trustee or creditor then invokes the disposable income rule. In a few cases the people end up being turned down for the house or car and are required to pay more into the plan because of higher disposable income.

Section 17

Post Filing Steps and Problems in Chapter 7

The filing of the bankruptcy petition does not end the bankruptcy process. There are several events that regularly do occur and some that might occur after the petition is filed.

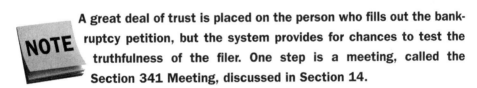 **A great deal of trust is placed on the person who fills out the bankruptcy petition, but the system provides for chances to test the truthfulness of the filer. One step is a meeting, called the Section 341 Meeting, discussed in Section 14.**

Audit

If there are questions about the filing, the trustee can order an audit. This can take several forms. The trustee may direct an appraiser to go out to a person's home and value the contents of the home. This is sometimes done when the filer has a very expensive home and puts a very low value on the furnishings in that home. Trustees have found, by experience, that people with very expensive homes tend to buy expensive, high quality furniture for those homes. (They may also send an appraiser to value vehicles. Sometimes old cars are not worth much at all, and sometimes they are valuable collector's items.)

In a business context, an audit or review by an appraiser is common. The greater likelihood of obtaining money from a sale makes this expense worthwhile for the trustee. Some courts have random audits. Here the trustee will require back-up to the statements in the bankruptcy petition. The filer will be asked to produce deeds and car titles (to see what type of car the filer really owns and who owns the land and the vehicle) and bank records (to see how much money is really flowing through the business and the individuals' hands), etc.

Challenges by the Creditors

One of the main safeguards in the system is that creditors can challenge the petition and the property of debt discharge. An important source of challenges by creditors is changes in the filer's borrowing and spending pattern. Sometimes people go on spending sprees just before filing their bankruptcy. They go on vacation or buy a large number of personal items. They then try to do away with these debts through bankruptcy. Creditors have the right to challenge discharge of these debts.

In the past, if a creditor gave a business or an individual a line of credit it was the creditor's problem if the borrower used it. The idea was, be sure who you are lending to and get security for your loans. Today the rules are a bit different. Borrowers on standing lines of credit—such as credit cards—are often deemed to be making a representation of their ability and intent to repay each time they draw or charge on their line of credit. If this representation is found to be false, the creditor can move to not allow the debt to be discharged. Some creditors try to abuse this new power by putting a "squeeze play" on borrowers. They challenge many charges and leave it up to the borrower to demonstrate their motives were pure when they borrowed.

The problem with this is that the final arbitrator of the borrower's intentions is a judge, and it is expensive to have a federal trial before a judge. This involves many filings and appearances before the court and extensive *discovery* (gathering of evidence). The creditor has "deep pockets" and the bankrupt is by definition without money. Some creditors use this situation to go on fishing expeditions. They threaten challenges and then offer to settle for a lesser sum. If they can threaten enough people and induce enough people to settle, they can collect a tidy sum across the country.

To stop this process from being abused, the law now provides that if the creditor brought a challenge without a reasonable basis, the creditor must pay the debtors attorney's fees. This does not happen in every case, but it happens enough that the creditors are dissuaded from making challenges without any basis in fact. Creditors will also ask why the assets and their values listed on loan applications are different from what is shown on the bankruptcy petition. If a great deal of money or assets has disappeared they will want to know what happened to it.

Challenges by Third Parties

Another element that makes the system work is that third parties often call the trustee's attention to improper action by the filer, unhappy business associates or ex-spouses are a fruitful source of negative information. Ex-employees also often know a lot and will call the trustee's attention to improper actions or assets that have not been listed. (There was even a case where a filer tried to hide assets by buying an expensive exempt asset, filed, and then returning the asset for a refund. The merchant, unhappy at losing the big sale, turned the filer in.)

Criminal Sanctions

If it comes out that a filer tried to lie to the trustee or to hide assets, the filer is subject to criminal *sanctions* of fines and time in jail. Every month brings stories of people fined and sent to prison for trying to hide assets or otherwise beat the system.

PART III

Life and Business
After
Filing Bankruptcy

Section 18

Continuing in Business *after* Bankruptcy

Many proprietors who run into money problems and have to consider going into bankruptcy are burnt out. They choose to give up running their own business and take a job as an employee. Others want to keep running a business and look for ways to do so after the bankruptcy. Whether they will be able to do so will depend on the nature of the business.

Any business has assets that may be lost in a bankruptcy, including ones you may not at first think of, such as business names, location, and phone numbers. If a customer is used to calling one place at a given phone number, or going to a specific location, and those elements are gone after the bankruptcy, the owner will face the challenge of reopening the business under a new name. As often happens, there is a period when the service or sales cannot be made, competitors may have moved in on the account and competition will be tougher.

Keeping a Business Alive

There is a great temptation to move tools and office equipment, particularly computers and software, away from the business location. As mentioned elsewhere, it is often not clear whether the business owns a computer, particularly a portable computer or software. This urge must be resisted. Hiding assets from the trustee, which includes moving material from one location or category to another, is bank-ruptcy fraud. It can easily lead to criminal prosecution and jail time. Do not expect your lawyer to help you do this. The lawyer has a duty to the court to make sure the system is not cheated of assets, and the lawyer could lose his or her license if he or she knowingly allows fraud.

Besides, it is not at all necessary to run such a risk to regain the tools and equipment. Office furniture is easy to replace. Your computer software and the records contained in them have almost no value to anyone else. For this reason, the trustee is likely to abandon them or sell them back to you for a very low price. In fact, the biggest danger is that the trustee, presuming that there is no value or utility in the software, will casually abandon it or have it destroyed. You can best help yourself here by letting the trustee know that you wish to have or buy these records and software.

Business Name

Your business name has a great deal of value. If your business was incorporated, the corporate name was listed with your state's secretary of state, and probably that particular name is protected. If you wish to keep it, you should make sure the old corporation is dissolved. This will free up the name. Then you can simply incorporate a new busi-ness with the same name, or otherwise file to protect the business or trade name. Remember, the trade or corporate name is an asset of the court, and if you have a particularly good business name, the trustee may try to sell it. Some names such as Skinny Dip for a yogurt store, Pair of Dice for a game store, or Hair Force for a hair salon may be so good that someone would be willing to pay the trustee to obtain the name. But, this is unlikely. There is no central exchange where people looking for business names can go, so it is hard for the trustee to find a buyer.

Business Phone Number

Another important asset of the business is the phone number. Your phone number is your life line as it is how most of your customers get in touch with you. Nothing signals that you are gone more definitely than the message, "this number has been disconnected," or for the caller to reach a private residence rather than your business.

For example:

> Several years ago we moved our office from one part of town to another, far enough away that the phone company made us use a different phone number. We let all the clients we could think of know about our new phone number. Still, our business fell off. When this happens one never knows if it is caused by seasonal adjustments, overall business climate, or "sun spot" activity. But, by sheer chance we learned that our old phone number had been assigned to the child of a man we used to work with.

> After about a year and a half, he told us that it was a real problem for his son. The son was getting phone calls meant for us all the time, and his answering machine was being filled up with messages meant for us. This one in a million set of circumstances let us see both sides of how important a phone number can be. We were wondering where our business had gone, and the boy was being aggravated by unwanted business calls.

If you want to continue your phone service, the answer is once again fairly simple. The phone number has absolutely no value to the trustee and he or she will likely sell it to you for a normal price or just allow you to have it back. You must, in addition, be sure that the monthly bill is paid to the phone company so they do not cut off service, and that they record the formalities of moving ownership from the corporation to you or your new company.

Business Location

Location, location, location can also be important to your business. Many businesses want to keep on operating in the same location, as that is where their customers know to find them. In addition, most businesses draw their customers from a specific geographic area. Simply put they come to you because you are convenient. If you move to another part of town they will find a new store, cleaner, bookkeeper or whatever.

It is possible to keep the same location, but it does involve a bit more risk and trouble. If the corporation owns the building and/or land, it will be very difficult to keep the same location. This normally has value and a ready market into which the trustee can sell. You, on the other hand, likely do not have any money to buy it from him.

Life is easier if the space is leased. The space is normally a liability to the trustee, as he has to keep on paying the rent if he is going to try to sell the lease. The market for such a sale may be narrow as most leases limit subleases and what businesses can be operated in the space. Normally the trustee will give up his or her right to the space fairly casually.

The landlord may be more of a problem. You very well may have had a slow, or no payment history with him or her for a period while the business was going down hill. He or she may not be that interested in having you continue as a tenant and may in fact be happy to be rid of you without having to go through the legal steps of evicting you. On the other hand, it is a lot easier on him or her to have you in the space. He or she has little down time in receiving rent, and will not have to do any "upfitting". If you want to stay in the same location by all means talk to the landlord. It's just business to him or her and often you will be surprised at what a landlord is willing to do with you if you can present a realistic case on how you can pay in the future.

Creditors and Other Problems

But remember, there are problems with keeping everything—location, name, phone number—the same. Creditors are likely to feel that the bankruptcy was just a sham. They may continue too make collection efforts against you as the proprietor. It can be very difficult to explain to them or the court that now you are not the same entity.

Another problem with continuing the business after the bankruptcy is that for a period the business will be closed. In a Chapter 7, operations must stop and the assets are sealed. To avoid a "Going out of Business" sign, most proprietors put out a more ambiguous sign such as "Closed for Inventory," "Closed for Remodeling" or even "Closed for Vacation." Of course, this does not fool anyone who is closely monitoring the location for very long. But it may help with casual customers who come by only once every month or two, as by the time they come back you are back in business.

It always surprises us how often people just drop in on a business when they are out driving or running errands. These people, not having an appointment or a real specific mission in visiting your operation, are not put off by finding the business is not in operation that day. Then it will often be several months until chance or their schedules cause them to come back by the business location.

Section 19
Rebuilding Credit

People who have gone through a financial storm normally have one of two reactions—they never want to obtain credit again, or they wonder if they can ever get credit in the future.

Reasons to have Credit

Some clients say, "I never want to see another credit card or owe anything." While understandable, this may be an overreaction and counter productive. While one can exist just fine without a credit card one will sooner or later need a car, or will have to move and buy a new home or rent an apartment. To do any of these things will require a reasonable credit rating. If one does nothing about rebuilding their credit standing one may not be able to qualify for the car, home or apartment. Credit is much like a muscle—it must exercise—to be available when needed. So go ahead and work on developing your credit standing and use your credit a little bit. In that way you will have a good credit record should you ever need it.

Obtaining Credit after Bankruptcy

There is a common misconception that people who have filed bankruptcy can never receive credit again. Rest assured—you can have credit again. There is too much profit for financial institutions to make to cut you off from credit for very long. If you can obtain credit, how long will it be before institutions will extend credit, and what can be done to shorten the time?

Time

It is hard to give a firm rule on how long it will take to receive credit again. There is not a law saying when you are again entitled to credit—it is up to the individual bank or business. And there are millions of banks and creditors in the country. Some are liberal in extending credit. Others will pass up a sale or loan if you ever filed bankruptcy. All that can be done is to describe averages.

Time is one of your great allies. The longer ago your bankruptcy, the less it will affect you. Most of the time, within two to five years you should be well on your way back to having a normal credit rating. It will go a bit faster if you have been working hard on rebuilding your credit—a bit slower if you didn't try to rebuild your credit. The two to five year number is for mainstream credit cards. It will take longer to be back to an A-rating in applying for a home.

Reaffirming Credit Cards

It is not easy to obtain new credit. If regaining access to credit takes time and is hard, why not *reaffirm* some of the debts you had prior to bankruptcy? This will let you keep one or more of your relationships with old lenders. All you have to do is pay off the balance you owe on the debt, and you have a credit card you can charge on, or a loan company to go to for future loans.

The main reason bankruptcy lawyers counsel against this course of action is that you need to get your financial feet under you before you start using credit again. A secondary reason is that often people want to reaffirm a larger debt than they can pay given their current financial situation. And remember that often the creditor will cut off your access to its credit line after you reaffirm. You end up with the debt and do not have the use of the card or credit line.

Let's discuss the reaffirmation process. Say you owe $2,000 on a credit card. You would sign an agreement, or note in your bankruptcy petition, that you will promise to pay the debt in spite of having the right to wipe it out as part of the bankruptcy process. The implied trade off for your doing this is that you will get to keep the card and use it in the future. However, some credit cards issuers will revoke the card once a customer files bankruptcy. So reaffirming the card merely means you have taken forward a debt you did not have to pay and will receive no benefit for your act.

If the bank does not revoke the card they will almost certainly lower your credit to what you owe. Thus if you owe $2,000 then your credit limit is lowered to $2,000. In effect you cannot use the card to charge anything until you pay off part of the $2,000. And remember, making the minimum payments each month will not make the balance go down much at all. You will need to make monthly payments that are a good bit larger than the minimum payment to obtain use of the card.

Meanwhile do not forget you are starting out at your credit limit. It is very easy to slip up and have an over the limit charge applied against you. These charges are becoming larger and larger as lenders search for more ways to make money. The fact that you are at the limit because you reaffirmed the debt and had your limit lowered will not make one bit of difference to the computer that is doing the "over the limit" calculations.

The most important reason to think long and hard about reaffirming a credit card debt is you, in all likelihood, will not be able to pay down the debt fast enough to use the card. Most people who file Chapter 7 do not have any money left over from their paycheck after their living expenses are deducted. In fact, most have living expenses higher than their monthly income. The factor that is allowing them to survive month to month is that insurance and taxes do not have to be paid each month and clothes are bought irregularly.

Taking on another bill may be the "straw that breaks their backs." If they run into repayment problems on the reaffirmed debt they are in real trouble. Having a bad pay history after bankruptcy is worse than having one prior to the bankruptcy. It shows you have not learned your lesson.

If you do have extra funds left over after paying your living expenses, you can afford to pay down a credit card, and if you have a real need for credit, then think about reaffirming a debt or two. Choose which one to reaffirm carefully. It is far better to reaffirm a credit card with a $500 limit than one with a $2,000 limit. Your goal is to have a credit card or two to use and to rebuilt your credit, not to be able to brag about how much credit you have available.

Next, be sure the one you keep is one that reports to the credit bureaus. Some department stores do not report to the credit bureaus. Pick a major credit card—Visa, Master Card. Those will be reported, and having one can help you get the right department store and gas company credit card when the proper time comes.

Score Keeping

If you are serious about rebuilding your credit in the fastest possible time, you need to learn how your credit rating is determined.

Much of the credit rating in this country is done by a California company named Fair, Isaac and Company. It licenses its program to determine creditworthiness to the big three credit bureaus and other businesses that may want to determine whether or not to make loans.

Fair, Isaac was one of the first and best companies to use complex mathematical algorithms, crunched on computers to predict borrowers' future actions. The people at Fair, Isaac are very smart and very good at analyzing numbers. In 1999 they were hired by NASA to "identify, analyze and track the root causes of ground processing anomalies in space shuttle missions" (Fair, Isaac press release October 25, 1999). Thus the rocket scientists go to Fair, Isaac for help.

Developing consumer financial profiles produces a large part of the company's $270—$280 million revenue. To protect this income stream it has tried hard to keep the factors that are considered in it's algorithms and how they are multiplied a secret. For this reason, anyone writing on credit rebuilding prior to June 2000 relied purely on intuition, observation, and guess work.

Fair, Isaac scores are used by about 75% of the country's mortgage lenders and all three major credit bureaus. Each bureau has its own name for the score, but at the bottom they are based on the Fair, Isaac

Score. The Fair, Isaac Score is called a FICO score (short for Fair, Isaac Company Score). These scores have been used for decades in consumer loans and credit cards under a heavy veil of secrecy. But, controversy developed as the score method moved into the mortgage industry. All aspects of people's lives were being controlled by a small group in California without accountability and in total secrecy.

The reason Fair, Isaac gave for its action and the secrecy was that the public needed more than their score—they needed additional information and individual counsel from a lender to truly understand their credit standing and how to improve it. (Craig Watts, Fair, Isaac's Consumer Affairs Manager). This ignored the fact that no lender was giving any additional information to the consumer to tell them how to improve their score in the eyes of anyone.

In fact, Fair, Isaac's entire business depends on this information not coming out. If consumers know how the scores work they can change their actions and standing and undercut the predictive value of the product the company is selling. Likewise, if the information gets out competitors can gain insight into the formulas and factors that the company is selling.

This raw display of power created a disturbance and at last state governments and the Federal Trade Commission ("FTC") got involved. The California Senate began to consider whether to pass a law to make Fair, Isaac reveal all. In July 1999, Fair, Isaac made a presentation of some of the factors used in determining a consumer's credit score. They gave examples of twelve factors and how differences in them would give different points. The higher the score, the more credit-worthy one is.

	Own	Rent	Other	No Info				
Own/Rent	25	15	10	17				
Years at Address	<.5	.5-2.49	2.5-6.49	6.5-10.49	>10.49	No Info.		
	12	10	15	19	23	13		
Occupation	Pro	Semi-Pro	Manager	Office	Blue Col.	Retired	Other	No Info.
	50	44	31	28	25	31	22	27
Years on Job	<.5	.5-1.49	1.5-2.49	2.5-5.49	5.5-12.49	12.5	Retired	No Info.
	2	8	19	25	30	39	43	20
Depart. Store/Maj. Cred. Cards	None	Dept. Store	Major CC	Both	No Answer	No Info.		
	0	11	16	27	10	12		
Bank Reference	Checking	Savings	Check. and Sav.	Other	No Info.			
	5	10	20	11	9			
Debt Ratios	<15	15-25	26-35	36-49	50+	No Info.		
	22	15	12	5	0	13		
Number Inquiries	0	1	2	3	4	5-9	No Rec.	
	3	11	3	-7	-7	-20	0	
Years in File	<.5	1-2	3-4	5-7	8+			
	0	5	15	30	40			
Number of Revolving Trades	0	1-2	3-5	6+				
	5	12	8	-4				
% Balances Available	0-15%	16-30%	31-40%	41-50%	>50%			
	15	5	-3	-10	-18			
Worst Credit Derog	No Record	Any Derog	Any Slow	1 Satisf. Line	2 Satisf. Lines	3 Satisf. Lines		
	0	-29	-14	17	24	29		

(The first line in each block is the individuals' status. The second line is the points allocated for that status.)

For more information see the FTC website at www.FTC.gov. Clearly these are not all the factors. Fair, Isaac once stated even a simple credit scoring system is likely to have 10,000 or 20,000 different possible combinations. The total scores range from 300 to 900 points.

So the few elements given in the government briefing cover only a part of this possible score range.

Fair, Isaac claims it uses only financial information in its credit scoring formula. Factors such as part of town lived in, race, sex or nationality are not considered. Others doubt this—Fair, Isaac once said age was not considered and yet the data presented by it at the briefing uses years in the credit file as a proxy, and one of their slides lists age as a factor in evaluating the credit applicant.

As you look at the sample chart there are many factors you cannot effect in your efforts to rebuild your credit standing. But, there are several things you can do:

- Stay at one address and do not move around.
- Be careful when you do obtain credit to make timely payments.
- If you have a job, do not hop around.
- If you are running your own business you may wish to consider taking a part time job so your report shows employment with the steady income.

You can obtain a copy of your FICO score by using the Internet. This is obtained through a website maintained by Fair, Isaac and one maintained by Equifax. The Fair, Isaac site is **www.myfico.com**. They do not go out of their way to make it easy and some search engines and Web systems will not work with these sites. You may have to try several different search engines before you find one that works.

Rebuilding Your Credit

There are a number of steps you can take to rebuild your credit. Read this section closely for the best ones you should take first.

Make Sure You have Clean Credit Reports

While you are working on rebuilding your credit, you will need to keep a sharp eye on your credit report. The FICO score uses information in your credit report so you will want to make sure it is up to date and accurate. Be sure to order a credit report from each of the three major credit reporting agencies as information on them can be different and you never know which one a potential credit extender will use. The phone numbers are:

Equifax 800-997-2493

Trans Union 800-888-4213

Experian 888-397-3742.

These numbers can change. If one of these numbers does not work call 800 information (800-555-1212) for the current number. The cost for each credit report normally runs about $8.00.

It will be tempting to order over the Internet. Be careful as these often contain listings from several credit agencies. If there is an error you will not know who to go to in order to correct the mistake and mistakes are fairly common. The credit bureaus are private companies that rely on what other private companies tell them for the most part. Common errors are to have data for other people in your file, and to not show a debt as paid off or discharged in bankruptcy. Order your credit report and go over it with a fine tooth comb.

Fix errors

If there is an error, be sure to write to correct it. Send a copy of your bankruptcy discharge letter and list of creditors if a debt is not shown as discharged. Challenge debts that are not yours or that are wrong. To do this, write to the credit bureau and challenge the history and asked that the entry be researched. By law the bureau must go back to the reporting company and ask for documentation of the entry. Ideally the company will look at its records and note the entry is wrong and have it corrected. Often the company will not bother to respond. If they do not, the entry must be taken off your credit report.

Every three to six months order another copy of your credit report. This will allow you to track how your credit rebuilding efforts are working. After you are sure you have cleaned up any errors, a combined credit report over the Internet will work fine.

Check Court Records

Often people who had judgments against them have paid them off, but the court records do not show it. People just assume that once they have paid the debt the judgment will disappear. This is often not the case. The court system has no way of knowing if you paid off a judgment or not. For a judgment to be marked satisfied, someone, normally the judgment holder, must advise the court system that the judgment has been paid.

Many creditors simply do not bother to do this. They have their money and that is what they are interested in. To get in touch with the court is extra work that is not producing a profit—so why do it?

It is up to you to be sure that paid-off judgments are removed from the court records. First check the judgment book at the court house for the court that entered the judgment. Be sure each judgment is marked "satisfied." It is very important to have judgments shown as paid, as unpaid judgments are automatically picked up by the credit agencies and hurt your credit score.

If a judgment has not been marked as paid you will need to get in touch with the creditor and have it report to the court that the judgment was satisfied. Often the best you can get from the creditor is a note that says the judgment was paid. You will have to do the leg work of getting this information to the court house.

Work to Rebuild Your Credit

The first step is to realize that your credit rating is not a reflection of your worth as a person. Rather a credit rating is at bottom a statement of how likely a lender is to make money off of you. To determine this they look at several factors. First, are other companies making money off of you? That is, do you have other debts and are you paying them regularly and on time? We cannot over emphasize the importance of having paid on time.

Next, do you have blemishes on your record—have you had foreclosures, repossessions, bankruptcy and charge offs? Third, are you stable? Do you have ties to the community and a regular job? Like a bail bondsman, lenders want to know how likely you are to skip town and how easy you will be to find. Fourth, do you have a regular flow of income? A nice job with a regular income is best. Worst is no job. Somewhere in between is being self-employed. At best a self-employed person or small businessperson has an irregular income, up some months and years and down in others. When the income is down it will be hard—if not impossible—to make the regular payments that bankers want.

However, be careful who you go to for credit and how you do it. There is a feeling among people who study the art of rebuilding credit that going to high interest credit cards, sub-prime markets, or even finance companies will not help you much, and may even hurt you. Therefore, be careful of credit card solicitations you receive while you are in bankruptcy or just after you come out of bankruptcy. These are often high interest, high charge cards.

Credit for a fee

Be especially careful of letters offering to obtain a credit card for you for a fee. Often the only thing these companies are interested in obtaining is your fee. They will forward your application to several credit card companies—often high interest ones. You could do the same thing yourself with a little research. The result: you will be out of pocket money you did not need to spend. In addition, you will have a large number of credit inquiries on your credit record (a FICO negative) and will probably end up with only offers to extend credit from a high interest card.

As you apply for credit, be careful in dealing with lenders that do not get too many credit inquiries on your record. What many people do when they want to re-establish their credit standing is send out a number of inquiries and hope that one will be accepted. But, unfortunately, the very act of sending out applications to several lenders lessens their chances of being accepted. Look at line eight on the FICO scoring chart. The lowest score you can get is to have more than five inquiries. The chart does not say over what time period, but you can be sure many inquiries over a month or so will not look good on your permanent record.

Phones

While much of a FICO score is beyond your control, there are some things you can affect. One of the first things you should do is have a phone in your name. It is not unusual for people during their run to bankruptcy to have their phone service cut off because they were not able to pay their phone bill.

A phone in most places is considered a public utility and the company will have to provide your phone service and can cover the credit risk requiring a deposit. The amount of the deposit will vary. In our area it is two months' average usage. Thus, if your habit was to make a lot of long distance charges your deposit will be higher than if you made only local calls. View paying the deposit as a cost of being in the game and pay what is required. Whatever they ask try to get a phone. Lack of a phone shows a lack of stability and this will hurt you as you try to rebuild your credit.

Be careful of phone services that cater to people who have phone service cut off. Using them will place you in a pool of credit risks and just may work against you. Work on obtaining phone service from your mainline phone company.

Bank accounts

Next open a bank checking and savings account. Be careful in doing this if you do not already have one, or must move. Many banks will not open a new account for people who have bounced checks. Some banks will not open checking accounts for people who have bad credit. This is not a universal practice, but it has happened on occasion. If you are opening a new account talk to the bank officer and ask what the bank's policy is. A turn down for a checking or savings account probably will not be reported to the credit bureaus and thus would not hurt you—but why take a chance?

Secured bank loans

After you have a savings and checking account at your bank, start thinking about a secured loan from that bank. This is where you have, say, $500 in your savings account, and you obtain a loan of $400 or $500. The bank will put a lock on your money, so if you do not pay, the loan is fully protected. It might at first seem like this type of loan would be easy to obtain because the bank is protected. But, you must keep in mind how loan officers are graded. If they make a loan that goes bad it is a black mark on their record and hurts their chances of promotion. So the loan officer is likely to be careful about making a loan to you. This is another case where you should talk with the bank officer to try to find out ahead of time if he or she will make the loan.

Remember, the bank will request data from the credit bureaus in considering the loan and too many inquiries will hurt you. You want each inquiry to result in a loan. It is extra work to take the time to sit down and talk with the loan officer, but you have had a financial mishap and will probably need to do the work if you want to speed up your credit availability.

Once you have the secured loan make sure you pay it back on time. Your goal is to have a satisfactory line on your credit report for that loan for the FICO scorekeepers to take into account. We suggest that you do not use the loan at all—bank it so you will be sure to have the money to pay back the loan as it comes due. You may ask yourself, "If I cannot use the loan what good is it?" It's purpose is to gain you a good post bankruptcy rating on your credit report. The loan interest you pay on the loan is the price you pay for the good entry. You are starting to rebuild a record on lenders making money off of you.

You might even be able to talk the bank into loaning you the money it puts a hold on. This is hard to do as it seems to go against everything bank officers believe in. But, if you are lucky, you will obviously be able to borrow more and have a lower loan repayment on your record.

Secured credit cards

Another source of secured loans is secured credit cards. These work in much the same way as a secured bank personal loan. You deposit, for instance, $500 in the bank who issues the secured credit card and your credit limit on the card is $500. Secured credit cards used to be a bit hard to find, but if you have access to the Internet it is now somewhat easier.

Before you settle on one, ask the banks how long it will be until your credit limit is lifted beyond what you have deposited in their bank. This assumes you have a perfect payment history. Some banks no matter how well you do will not give you unsecured credit. Your job is to find the ones that will.

You may receive offers in the mail for secured credit cards. Be very careful in accepting these—going with companies that offer these credit cards can work against you. An easy way to find secured credit cards is through the Internet—but this may not be the best way. This is just another way of making a mass offering—similar to mail solicitations. Be careful.

Before you sign up call and ask some important questions.

- Do they report to the major credit bureaus, if so which ones?
- Do they report your card as a secured credit card? If they do it will probably not help you in rebuilding your credit. Even if they say they do not check up on them. This is one of the things you should review when you order follow up credit reports.
- How long is your grace period on monthly payments? Too short a grace period will cause you to pay extra interest. The worst is interest accruing from the date of charge.
- Is there an application fee? The lower the fee the better.
- What is the minimum and maximum deposit required or allowed in setting up an account? A low balance can create just as successful a payment entry as a high one.
- With a good payment history, how long will it take to be chargeable into an unsecured credit card? Aim for twelve to eighteen months.
- How much of the deposit is available for use on the credit card? You don't want to give a security deposit of $1,000 and have a credit card line of $500.
- What is the interest rate on outstanding balances? Some banks will charge a very high interest rate. All other things being equal, lower is better.
- Is there an annual service fee? None or low is better but hard to find.
- Do they pay interest on the security deposit that is made?
- Do they deal with people in your state? Some banks will not deal with out of state residents and others block out certain states.

Other things to look for are a toll-free customer service number and automated customer assistance. You will want to check your credit balances often to make sure you are not going over your limit, and it is nice to be able to check twenty-four hours a day.

If you have an IRS lien or owe back taxes, some banks may not give you a secured credit card. If you have this problem ask about their policy before sending any money.

Also ask about other rules: make sure the lender has a working phone number, a street address, income requirements and no on-going law suits. Sometimes it is possible to obtain an unsecured credit card but these often require high up front fees, offer a low credit line and charge high interest rates.

It takes time to process paperwork and money for a post bankruptcy secured or unsecured credit card. If you are in a hurry you should start early. Most banks will not issue a card until you have received your discharge papers, but you can start talking with them before you actually have the papers in your hand. Many will send out the application form prior to your receiving your discharge papers with the understanding that you must wait to send the application in until you receive the discharge. Most will want a copy of your discharge papers. You can speed the process up by sending a certified check or money order rather than a personal check.

When your secured card can be turned into an unsecured one will often depend on time—eighteen months, thirty-six months or whatever. Also your FICO score will depend in part on how long you have been making timely payments on your debts. So it makes sense to get an early start.

Remember your payment history only helps you if it is reported to a credit bureau—so ask if they report, and then after a few months order a copy of your credit report to be sure it is reported. You do not want to waste your time working with a bank that does not report to the credit bureaus.

Some banks that issue secured credit cards report to the credit bureau that the card is a secured card. It probably will not do you much good to dutifully pay on a credit card that is noted as secured in your credit file. Try hard to find a bank that does not report the fact that it is secured.

Credit Cards

You should think through why you are seeking a credit card. Is it a necessity? Making motel and airline reservations are often given as reasons why a person must have a credit card. Another reason is convenience. It is easier and safer to carry a credit card than a pocket full of cash. A third is to have a line of credit—a source of funds for an emergency.

Emergencies

It will be awhile before you will have the use of a credit card for a real source of funds for an emergency. If your reaffirm a credit card debt you will start off with a low credit line or no credit line at all. If you obtain a secured credit card the credit limit will be so low it will not be much help.

Convenience

Credit cards are convenient—perhaps too convenient. It is easy to whip out the plastic when you want to buy something without really thinking about the cost. That is what gets most of us in trouble. For day to day purchases a card is not really better than carrying cash and is inferior in one way. Most purchases such as dry cleaning, food, and gas are for reactively small amounts, less than $50 or $100. Carrying a few twenty dollars bills in your billfold would allow you to make these purchases. Credit cards are inferior to cash as using them is so easy we often forget we made a purchase.

Opening your billfold or your purse psychologically makes you think about the purchase. You are more likely to elect to pass the item up, or at least remember you already spent money when you are considering another purchase. Credit cards are of course absolutely necessary for ordering items over the Internet or by phone. However, most items purchased over the Internet or from a mail order catalog are not necessities. Not buying these items is a good place to start to bring your spending under control.

Building credit

For the next year or so, there is only one reason you want a credit card—to build a history of making your monthly payments on it in a timely way. Or put another way, to show the issuer that it will make money off of you. For this reason you will need to use your card for a few purchases, and not pay off the entire balance every month. People who pay off their entire balance each month do not pay any interest charges to the bank and thus the bank does not make any money off of them. They are known in the banking industry as "freeloaders" and some banks are instituting a monthly charge on people who never carry a balance over from month to month.

> **NOTE** The credit rating score (the FICO Score) explanation is careful never to mention this—but we believe it is an important part of bank decisions on who to issue credit cards to.

The banks naturally prefer someone who will make them money over someone who is a "freeloader." Think back to when you carried a large credit card debt over month to month. You likely received many credit card applications in the mail, and perhaps checks already made out to you ready to be cashed. You were an ideal customer, one who paid a minimum amount regularly each month, but who seldom paid off the entire balance so the bank received those nice checks month after month like clockwork. Perhaps the opposite of "freeloader" should be defined as "sucker."

Your goal is to, in a small way, replicate that profile—running a balance each month, paying regularly in a timely way without having a large balance. That is your real goal for the next few credit rebuilding years: to have a few credit cards that carry a modest balance while you establish a record of paying on time each month. Do not worry about how a credit card is more convenient, or a source of emergency funds. You should very deliberately and carefully charge just enough each month to keep an ongoing balance. The balance should be low. Look at the Fair, Isaac chart—you want to have an outstanding balance of less than 15% of your available credit for a maximum score in that category.

Gas Company Cards

Another credit card that will add to your rebuilt credit history is a gas card. You can greatly improve your chances of getting a gas company credit card if you own stock in the company. In effect your stock is the security for the card. Think about several things in taking this step. Pick a gas company that has stations where you will use them and is large enough to have stations where you will be traveling. Pick a company where the stock investment will be fairly safe—stocks can go down so you can lose part of your investment if you are not careful. You can buy your stock through a broker or, in some cases, directly from the company. Shop the major oil companies. As you call around ask to be sure the company issues gas cards to shareholders and how much stock you must buy. These factors change over time so there is no avoiding the work of making the calls.

The 800 information number (800-555-1212) is a good place to start in finding these numbers. When you call ask if and for how long you will be required to pay the card off in full each month. The normal process is you buy the stock and in a few months an application for a credit card will automatically be sent to you. Be sure the company reports to the credit bureaus to maximize your credit rebuilding.

Department Store Cards

Another source of credit is department store cards. Department stores come in all sizes—from national chains to small one- or two-store operations. Often they will be more liberal in offering credit cards than the major credit card issuers. If you choose to try to obtain a department store card, be careful to investigate it beforehand. A request for credit may very well cause an inquiry on your credit report, so be sure to first try to get an idea if they will accept you and issue a card. In addition, make sure they will report your timely payments to the Credit Bureau. You should look into department store credit cards as having both a major credit card and a department store card picks up extra FICO points.

Car Loans

You can control the number of credit card applications you send out, but there are cases when you have less control over the number of inquiries that are made. If you should try to buy a car and obtain financing you are on dangerous ground. It is the custom among car dealers to take your financial information and then shop your case among many lenders. This is known as *shot gunning*. The Fair, Isaac people say their formulas take shot gunning into account and compensate for it, so it does not hurt you.

When you are in the credit rebuilding stages and you need a vehicle, shop first for the financing then the vehicle. The normal way people who do not have to worry about their credit shop for a car is to visit several car dealers and find a car they like. Then they ask about financing. Having fallen in love with one car they are stuck with the dealer and its practices. The dealers may *shot gun* you.

What you should do is shop first for the financing and after you have nailed that down pick a car from what is available. One way to avoid too many inquiries is for you to obtain a copy of your credit report and show it to the financing manager early in your talks. You can then ask if then are likely to make a loan. You can also give him a copy of your FICO score. They will need to verify these later, but this is a good starting point. Tell the financing manager you are trying to avoid too many credit inquiries on your record.

Houses

Getting on track to buy a home can take longer than merely qualifying for a credit card. More money is at stake so lenders are more careful. There are several different elements to consider.

More in down payment

First, the more money you can give as a down payment the easier, and sooner, it will be until you can qualify for a home loan. It will be hard for several years to qualify for a 5% down loan—easier to qualify for a 20% down loan. Of course this is of limited help if you have recently filed bankruptcy, because by definition you have very little extra money for a down payment. Another idea is to try to obtain an FHA loan. They often will make loans with smaller down payments.

Owner financing

Owner financing is another possibility. In some cases a seller will finance either the entire mortgage or a portion of the mortgage. Most sellers want a clean sale, but sometimes sellers who are having trouble selling their home or who for tax reasons are looking for a stream of monthly payments will consider this type of transaction. It does not hurt to ask.

Land contract or lease with option

Another possibility is a land contract or a lease with an option to buy. We suggest you stay away from this type of transaction as too many things can go wrong and cause you to lose your payments. If you use this option, make sure you have your lawyer draw up the papers.

Mortgage brokers

Many people turn to *mortgage brokers* to find lenders. There are many good ones and just as many bad ones. Mortgage brokers are paid very well if the deal goes through and make nothing if the loan is not made. They are highly motivated to get the job done. Unfortunately, some will put you in sub-prime lending situations, often with balloon notes. We hear all the time of people who were told the deal would have one set of terms and then they set everything up to move into their new home after closing. Then they were presented with another set of terms at closing. Often they sign the new (worse) terms because they feel they have no option but to sign and move into the home. If you use a mortgage broker to find a loan, hire your own lawyer to review the proposed loan and to go to the closing with you.

You may be told to take the loan at these terms and after a year of good payments the terms will change. Do not depend on this happening. We see people all the time who have been told this and then cannot get the terms changed. Expect to wait at least three to six years before you can buy a house with normal financing. In the mean time, work on rebuilding your credit.

Self-employed

Self-employed people have a harder time as they have irregular income. This makes lenders uneasy. Having a harder time buying a home is one of the prices you pay for being your own boss.

If you are self-employed and really want to speed up rebuilding your credit, it is far easier and maybe wiser to obtain a job with a steady income. You miss the highs and the independence, but gain the steady cash flow. If you do not want to work for someone else, or cannot find the right job, then it is best to not try to push the credit rebuilding process.

Living without Credit

While their credit is rebuilding, people often worry about their ability to travel. Most motels and hotels are set up to have you guarantee your reservation with a credit card. However, it is possible to reserve rooms without a credit card, but it will be more work. Most chains have programs where you can prepay your first night's deposit as a security deposit. Policies vary by chain and by the individual operator so you will need to call both to be sure you have all your bases covered. The 800 information line (800-555-1212) will get you the chain's main number and they can give you the individual hotel or motel number.

Normally you will mail a check for the first night's rent (some require payment for the entire stay). There are often time windows within which the payment must be made so ask about how soon payment must be made. Life will be easier if you pay by cash or cashiers check, although personal checks are accepted by some (subject to being received far enough in advance to clear).

If you will be traveling a good bit, ask about programs for frequent uses. Often after a time of usage and good payments, users can guarantee reservations without a credit card or deposit. If you are using your regular credit card for guaranteeing room reservations, check to see how much they freeze. Often a lock for more than the room rate is put on the card to cover long distance phone calls, etc. You do not want to use up all your credit card limit with your reservation deposit.

Glossary

A

accelerate. When a debtor fails to meet a requirement of the loan (such as making timely payments) and the creditor calls for the entire loan balance to be paid at once.

accounts receivable. Money owed to a business or person that has not yet been paid.

automatic stay. An order issued by the bankruptcy court stopping collection action against the person or business that filed bankruptcy.

B

bankruptcy estate. The sum of the property and assets owned by the person or business who filed bankruptcy.

bankruptcy trustee. A person appointed by the court to protect the rights of creditors of the bankruptcy filer.

bought account. A debtor's promise to pay creates an expectation of future payments. The rights to these future payments can be purchased by a third party. The third party then becomes entitled to receive payments from the debtor.

C

Chapter 7. A type of bankruptcy filed by either a corporation or an individual. It provides for the cancellation of certain unsecured debts without a repayment plan and may, but often does not, call for the sale of some of the filer's assets.

Chapter 11. A type of bankruptcy filed by either a corporation or an individual (but normally by a corporation). It provides for the reorganization of the debts of the filer and provides for a plan of repayment of debts in whole or part.

Chapter 12. A type of bankruptcy for family farms.

Chapter 13. A type of bankruptcy filing for individuals with regular income. It provides for the repayment, in whole or part, of the individual debts through regular payments to a Chapter 13 trustee over a period of three to five years.

civil lawsuit. A lawsuit against a person or entity that does not carry a criminal penalty. Lawsuits to collect debts by individuals or entities are almost always civil rather than criminal and therefore a debtor is not in danger of going to jail.

collateral. Property that is promised by a borrower as security for a loan. (See lien).

contingent debt. A debt that you may have to pay if an agreed upon event takes place.

corporate shield. Protection whereby operating as a corporation (in most cases), protects officers, directors, and shareholders from *personal liability* for injuries to third parties and business debts of the corporation. (This is sometimes known as the "corporate veil.")

corporation. A type of legal entity set up under state law which is treated for many purposes as a separate person.

creditor. A person or business that has money owed to it.

credit rating. A score which states a person's or business's credit worthiness. It is often used in deciding whether or not to make a loan.

credit report. A report produced by a credit bureau showing a person's or business's debts and repayment history.

D

debtor. A person or business that owes money to another.

default. The failure by a debtor to act as required in a loan contract. This is normally a failure to make payments on a debt when due.

dischargeable debt. Debts that can be cancelled in a bankruptcy.

discharge of debts. A bankruptcy court action or order which cancels certain debts and forbids creditors from making efforts to collect the discharged debts.

E

equity. The value of a piece of property after deducting liens.

ERISA (Employee Retirement Income Security Act). A 1970's era law that aims to protect employee retirement funds. It sets conditions that sponsors (normally employers) must meet to claim tax benefits for contribution to a retirement or other benefit program.

exempt property. Property a debtor is allowed to keep in bankruptcy.

F

foreclosure. A legal process whereby a lien holder (mortgage holder) moves to take land and any buildings on it.

freeze. In a financial transaction a freeze takes place when a person or entity holding funds refuses to release those funds because of a breach by the owner of the funds. For example, when a debtor fails to pay a loan to a bank, and the bank holds on to money in the debtors savings account.

H

hardship withdrawal. The right to withdraw funds from tax qualified pension or retirement savings when an unexpected emergency occurs or there is a pressing need for the funds.

home equity loan. A loan secured by an interest in the borrower's home. It creates a mortgage against the home.

J

judgment. An order of a court. If the order states that money is owed it is a *money judgment.*

judgment lien. A money judgment that attaches against property. The judgment lien must be paid when the home is sold or refinanced. It is possible in some cases to remove a judgment lien in a bankruptcy.

judgment proof. A person or business that has no assets a creditor can reach to collect court awarded judgments. In most states, a debtor may protect a certain amount of assets despite the fact that a creditor has a judgment against the debtor. If the debtor's assets are within the protected limits, the creditor may not collect on the judgment.

L

lead time. A period of time in advance of an expected action or event. It is normally used to prepare for the expected action or event or to perform an action.

leasor. An individual or entity which allows the use of property in exchange for periodic payments. Most commonly a person or entity allowing use of a vehicle or an apartment in exchange for monthly payments.

lien. A claim by a creditor against property of the debtor to insure that a debt is paid. Common examples of liens are loans secured by a claim against a vehicle and mortgages on homes.

M

meeting of creditors (also known as a 341 meeting). A bankruptcy hearing where creditors and the trustee are allowed to question a bankruptcy filer about his financial affairs.

money judgment. A court order directing the payment of money.

mortgage. A lien or claim against real property given to a creditor. The most common usage is a claim against ones home in exchange for the lending of money.

P

partnership. A joining by two or more individuals to achieve a goal, such as running a business. The partnership may be formal, created by signed agreements, or informal, with no written documents. General partners are personally liable for all partnership debts.

personal guarantee. A promise by a person or business to pay a debt that is not backed by a security interest. Often it is a promise to pay a debt if another person does not pay it. It makes the person giving the guarantee fully responsible for any portion of the debt that is not paid to the lender.

petitioner. A person or corporation that has filed a bankruptcy.

piercing the corporate veil. In some cases, if corporate shareholders and/or officers have acted improperly or failed to follow corporate formalities, the protection offered by the corporate shield can be lifted.

plan. In bankruptcy it is the written description filed by an individual or a corporation describing how debts will be treated. Bankruptcy plans are used in Chapter 11 and Chapter 13 bankruptcy filings.

process server. One who delivers lawsuit papers. Can be law enforcement personnel or an authorized private individual. The term normally refers to a private individual.

property. An item that has value. It can be land, accounts receivable, investments, household or business goods, vehicles, land, etc.

proprietors. A person who owns or operates a business.

prorate. A method of sharing funds among several people or entities according to a set criteria.

Q

quick ratio. As used in this book it is the total of unsecured debts divided by one year's disposable income. In financial analysis it is cash, marketable securities and accounts receivable divided by current liabilities.

R

reaffirmation agreement. Agreement signed by a bankruptcy petitioner stating he will continue paying a given debt owed to a creditor after the bankruptcy is completed. This is normally done for one of three reasons: a sense of moral obligation; to keep access to credit offered by a creditor (as in credit cards); or to keep collateral such as a vehicle which is subject to repossession.

real estate. Land with or without buildings on it. (also called *real property.*)

repossession. The taking of property that has been pledged as security or as collateral for the repayment of a loan. A repossession can be done with or without a court order.

right of off-set. The ability of a person or business that holds another's money (like a bank) to apply the money being held to a debt that is owed to that person or business. For example, a bank can apply money from your account to an overdrawn check on your account.

S

secured debt. A debt that is backed or secured by a claim on property. Examples are mortgages, claims against vehicles or accounts receivable.

security interest. The claim or lien on an item of property or an asset created by an agreement between a debtor and a creditor. This is different from a judgment lien or a tax lien created by a court or action of law.

senior lien. An item of property may have more that one claim against it. The senior lien is the one that must be paid or satisfied first. An example is a first mortgage where there is a first and second mortgage.

service of lawsuit papers. The delivery of a complaint or other lawsuit papers. This starts a law suit against the defendant. Lawsuit papers can be served by certified mail, a sheriff or other legal officer, or by a process server.

sole proprietorship. A business owned or operated by an individual that is not incorporated on part of a partnership.

statement of intentions. A declaration in a bankruptcy petition stating how secured and other debts will be treated.

statutory lien. A claim created by a statute or operation of the law. A common example is a tax lien against property.

stockholder. One who owns an interest in a corporation.

T

tax lien. A claim by a tax authority against property because of an overdue tax debt or obligation.

trade creditors. An individual or entity that has provided credit to a business.

trustee. A person or entity that has a claim on property for the benefit of a third party. Common examples are a trustee in connection with a home mortgage or a bankruptcy trustee. In bankruptcy the term is used to refer to the bankruptcy trustee.

U

unsecured debt. A debt not secured by an interest in an item of property or an asset.

unsecured loan. A promise by an individual or entity to pay a debt that is not backed by a security interest.

W

wage earner plan (or wage earner bankruptcy). Another name for a Chapter 13 bankruptcy.

wage garnishment. The taking of all or part of a debtor's wages for the benefit of a creditor. The employer takes the wages earned by the debtor and sends it to the creditor. This is done for private non-governmental creditors only after a money judgment. Government creditors can have a wage garnishment put in place without a court order.

wild card (or wild card exemption). The right to protect from creditors or a bankruptcy trustee any item of property up to a set dollar value.

workout (or workout program). An arrangement to pay a debt after the debt has gone into default.

Appendix A
Personal and Business Budgeting

Personal Budget—Family of four

This budget is based on household operating income. To get household operating income you would take after-tax income and deduct:

    1) Child support and alimony payments.

    2) Student loans and criminal restitution payments.

    3) Tuition and living expenses for family members at colleges and private schools.

Percentage of household operating income spent on each category:

Housing 20–40%
    (Includes mortgage payments, rent, heat, electricity, etc.)

Food 10–20%

Transportation 15–20%
    (Includes vehicle payment, gas and oil, etc., vehicle insurance, bus fare and saving for a replacement vehicle.)

Clothing 5–15%

Recreation, Church and Charitable Giving . . .5–20%
    (Includes vacations)

Medical, dental and personal care 5–10%
    (If you have a serious medical problem this could be far higher.)

The astute reader will note that these percentages can add up to more than 100%. Therefore, to live without resorting to borrowing, a family must trade off high spending in one area with low spending in other areas.

NOTE The above budget does not have a category for repayment of credit cards and personal loans. If debt payment is too large a percentage of your household operating income, you must cut back on outflows in other areas (food, transportation, etc.) or face the real possibility of eventual default.

Debt

How much debt is too much? The traditional rule of thumb was that your debt repayments should not exceed a third of the money you have left over after subtracting the money spent in the above categories from your household operating income.

Another traditional general guideline is that your total general debts (other than house and car loans) should not be larger than 20% of your household operating income for the year.

Business Budget

What a given business needs to spend in different areas (office space, helpers, advertising, supplies, transportation, fees, etc.) varies so much from business to business that a guideline for expenditures in each different area cannot be given. An accountant is likely to have expenses for office space, supplies, helpers and ongoing education, but might have a low percentage of her business expenses directed towards advertising and transportation.

A plumber on the other hand might have high expenses for helpers, advertising, and transportation, but spend little on office space. A courier's main expense would be transportation and she likely would spend little in the other areas.

However, despite these variations, most small business people use a general guideline of trying to limit the sum of these to 50% of business income.

Appendix B
Federal and State-Specific Bankruptcy Exemptions

Throughout the text of this book, there are several references to various *exemptions* one can take in bankruptcy. These are dollar amounts and limits on certain items (i.e. your home, vehicles, etc.) that cannot be used to pay your creditors. Listed in this appendix are both federal exemptions and any state-specific ones. Refer to your state first, and on page 172, there is a list of states that allow your choice of federal or your state's exemptions.

Federal Bankruptcy Exemptions

*The dollar amounts are indexed and will change each year.

Homestead up to:	$16,150.*
Vehicle up to:	$ 2,575.*
Personal Property up to:	$425* of value in one item, or $8,625* is aggregate value.
Tools of Trade:	$1,625.*
Wages:	Seventy-five percent of earned but unpaid wages.

Pension and Retirement Benefits: Certain Federal retirement benefits and ERISA qualified benefits.

Miscellaneous: Unemployment benefits, social security and public assistance. Most alimony and child support. Some life insurance values. Up to $1,075* in value of jewelry held primarily for personal use by debtor or a dependent. Aggregate interest in any property up to $850* plus up to $8,075* of any unused amount of the Homestead property.

Federal exemptions can be used as an alternative to state exemptions by residents of the following states and the District of Columbia:

Arkansas
Connecticut
District of Columbia
Hawaii
Massachusetts
Michigan
Minnesota
New Jersey
New Mexico
Pennsylvania
Rhode Island
South Carolina
Texas
Vermont
Washington
Wisconsin

State Exemptions

Alabama

Homestead up to:	160 acres worth no more than $5,000.
Vehicle up to:	(Included below in personal property.)
Personal Property up to:	$3,000.
Tools of Trade:	Military equipment.
Wages:	75% of wages earned but not paid at time of bankruptcy filing.
Pension and Retirement Benefits:	Unemployment benefits and workers' compensation, state employees' pensions and various other benefits.
Miscellaneous:	Certain insurance payments and business partnership property (as to personal debts).

Alaska

Homestead up to:	$54,000.
Vehicle up to:	Up to $3,000, if value of the vehicle is not over $20,000.
Personal Property up to:	Health aids, tuition credits, pets up to $1,000, $1,000 of jewelry and household goods, clothing, books, musical instruments, and family portraits and heirlooms up to $3,000.

(continued)

Tools of Trade:	Up to $2,800.
Wages:	Up to $350 per week or $550 if the household's only wage earner.
Pension and Retirement Benefits:	Public employees' pensions and ERISA qualified benefits.
Miscellaneous:	Most public benefits, alimony and child support in certain situations some insurance payments and business partnership property.

Arizona

Homestead up to:	$100,000.
Vehicle up to:	$1,500 ($4,000 if handicapped).
Personal Property up to:	$4,000 of assorted furniture, some livestock and some household items.
Tools of Trade:	Up to $2,500.
Wages:	Earnings of a minor child, unless the minor is the petitioner.
Pension and Retirement Benefits:	Pensions of some government officials and ERISA qualified benefits.
Miscellaneous:	Unemployment and welfare benefits, workers' compensation, child support and alimony, some life insurance policies and payments and business partnership property.

Arkansas

Homestead up to:

Head of Household may claim any amount if under 1/4 of an acre in a municipality or under eighty acres elsewhere. Up to $2,500 if between 1/4 of an acre and an acre in a municipality or between eighty and 160 acres elsewhere. Homestead exemptions do not apply to over one acre in municipalities or 160 acres elsewhere.

Others may claim real or personal property used as a residence up to $800 if single or $1,250 if married. A further $500 of personal property may be claimed if married or head of household, or $200 if single.

Vehicle up to:

Up to $1,200.

Personal Property up to:

$200 if single or $500 if married, clothing and wedding band with up to a 1/2 carat diamond.

Tools of Trade:

Up to $750.

Wages:

Earned but unpaid wages that have been due for over sixty days.

Pension and Retirement Benefits:

IRA deposits up to $20,000, if deposited a year before filing and school employees', police officers' and firefighters' pensions.

(continued)

Miscellaneous:	Unemployment benefits, workers' compensation, most crime victims reparations, some life insurance policies and payments and business partnership property.

California

(There are two different options for bankruptcy exemptions in California. The two systems cannot be mixed.)

Option 1

Homestead up to:	$50,000 if single, or $75,000 if a member of a family and no one else is claiming a homestead; or $125,000 if 65 or older or disabled; or if creditors are trying to force the sale of your home and you are single, 55 or older, and earn less than $15,000 per year; or if creditors are trying to force the sale of your home and you are married, 55 or older and earning less than $20,000 per year.
Vehicle up to:	Up to $1,900.
Personal Property up to:	All food, clothing, appliances, furnishings, and health aids. Home building materials up to $2,000 and jewelry and heirlooms up to $5,000 total.
Tools of Trade:	Up to $5,000.
Wages:	75% of wages earned thirty days prior to filing. *(continued)*

Pension and Retirement Benefits:	Public retirement benefits and private tax exempt retirement benefits.
Miscellaneous:	A burial plot, personal injury and wrongful death recoveries needed for support, unemployment and worker's compensation and most insurance benefits, health benefits and business partnership property.

Option 2

Homestead up to:	$15,000.
Vehicle up to:	$2,400.
Personal Property up to:	Clothing, household goods, appliances, furnishings, animals, books, musical instruments and crops up to $400 per item, health aids, jewelry up to $1,000, plus $800 worth of any property, and any unused portion of the $15,000 homestead exemption may be used to protect personal property.
Tools of Trade:	Up to $1500.
Wages:	————-
Pension and Retirement Benefits:	ERISA benefits needed for support.
Miscellaneous:	Unemployment, social security, welfare and veterans' benefits, crime victims' compensation, certain wrongful death and personal injury recoveries, alimony and child support needed for support, and some insurance policies and payments.

Colorado

Homestead up to:	$45,000 if occupied at time of filing.
Vehicle up to:	$3,000 if needed to get to work or up to $6,000 if an elderly or disabled person needs it to reach medical care.
Personal Property up to:	Clothing up to $1,500, health aids, household goods up to $3,000, food and fuel up to $600, one burial plot per person, up to $1,000 of jewelry, books and pictures up to $1,500.
Tools of Trade:	Stock in trade, supplies fixtures, machines, tools, maps, equipment and books up to $10,000. Library of a professional up to $3,000 and farm materials of a farmer up to $25,000.
Wages:	Minimum of 75% of wages.
Pension and Retirement Benefits:	ERISA benefits and public employees' pensions.
Miscellaneous:	Most personal injury recoveries, unemployment and workers' compensation, veterans' benefits, crime victims' compensation, AFDC aid to blind, aged and disabled, child support, some life insurance proceeds and business partnership property.

Connecticut

Homestead up to:	$75,000.
Vehicle up to:	$1,500.
Personal Property up to:	Food, clothing, health aids, appliances, furniture, bedding, wedding and engagement rings, plus $1,000 of any property.
Tools of Trade:	Military equipment, tools, books, instruments and farm animals.
Wages:	Minimum of 75% of wages.
Pension and Retirement Benefits:	State employees' pensions and past ERISA benefits.
Miscellaneous:	Municipal employees benefits, unemployment and worker' compensation, veterans' benefits, social security, crime victims' compensation, AFDC aid to the blind aged and disabled, health and disability benefits, life insurance proceeds and some unmatured policies.

Delaware

(Delaware allows $5,000 per person to protect real property, vehicle and personal property.)

Homestead up to:	General exemption per person.
Vehicle up to:	General exemption per person.

(continued)

Personal Property up to:	General exemption per person—clothing, jewelry, books, family pictures, piano, school books and family library, plus $500 of personal property if head of family.
Tools of Trade:	Tools, implements and fixtures worth up to $75 in New Castle and Sussex counties and up to $50 in Kent county.
Wages:	85% of earned unpaid wages.
Pension and Retirement Benefits:	State and Kent county employees', police and volunteer firefighters pensions and retirement plans.
Miscellaneous:	Most public benefits, private health and disability benefits and certain life insurance benefits.

District of Columbia

(These exemptions can be claimed by residents of D.C. or by those who earn the major portion of their livelihood in D.C.)

Homestead up to:	The debtor's aggregate interest in any residential condominium deposit.
Vehicle up to:	$2,575.
Personal Property up to:	$8,625 in household goods, animals, crops and musical instruments, but no one item may exceed $425 in value, any property worth up to $850 plus up to $8,075 in any unused homestead exemption, and professionally prescribed health aids.
Tools of Trade:	Up to $1,625.
Wages:	Up to $200 per month if the head of a family, otherwise, $60, and a minimum of 75% of earned, but unpaid wages.
Pension and Retirement Benefits:	Disability pensions needed for support, certain Federally approved retirement plans and judges' pensions.
Miscellaneous:	Most unmatured insurance policies, social security, veterans' benefits, disability, illness and unemployment benefits, alimony necessary for support, crime victims' reparations, wrongful death payments, some life insurance payments and compensation for pain and suffering.

Florida

Homestead up to:	Unlimited value, but not more than 1/2 an acre in a municipality or 160 acres elsewhere.
Vehicle up to:	$1,000.
Personal Property up to:	Health aids and up to $1,000 of any personal property.
Tools of Trade:	Included in personal property.
Wages:	Up to $500 weekly.
Pension and Retirement Benefits:	State and county employees', firefighters', teachers' and police pension plans, government deferred compensation plans, and certain plans found in the Internal Revenue code.
Miscellaneous:	Public assistance, social security, unemployment compensation, veterans' benefits, workers' compensation, crime victims compensation (in most cases), alimony and child support needed for support, most insurance proceeds and business partnership property.

Georgia

Homestead up to:	$10,000 (unused portion may be applied to other property).
Vehicle up to:	$3,500.
Personal Property up to:	$5,000 in household goods, clothes, books, musical instruments, animals and crops, no one item may be worth over $600. Jewelry up to $500, health aids plus a $600 "wild card" to protect any property.
Tools of Trade:	Up to $1,500.
Wages:	Minimum of 75%.
Pension and Retirement Benefits:	Public employees' pensions, ERISA benefits, and other pensions needed for support
Miscellaneous:	Most public benefits, some personal injury and wrongful death recoveries, alimony and child support needed for support, and certain life insurance policies.

Hawaii

Homestead up to:	$30,000 for heads of family and people over 65, $20,000 otherwise. Property cannot exceed one acre.
Vehicle up to:	$2,575.
Personal Property up to:	$1,000 for household goods including jewelry.

(continued)

Tools of Trade:	Needed for livelihood.
Wages:	100% for wages less than one month past due.
Pension and Retirement Benefits:	Public employees' pensions and ERISA qualified benefits deposited in the plan at least three years before filing.
Miscellaneous:	Unemployment and workers' compensation, Department of Public Safety assistance, disability benefits, certain life insurance benefits and business partnership property.

Idaho

Homestead up to:	$50,000.
Vehicle up to:	$3,000.
Personal Property up to:	$5,000 of household goods, but no one item valued over $500. Up to $1,000 of jewelry and up to $1,000 of crops cultivated on up to fifty acres.
Tools of Trade:	Up to $1,500 and all arms and equipment kept by peace officers and military personnel.
Wages:	Minimum of 75%.
Pension and Retirement Benefits:	Public employees' pensions and ERISA benefits, plus any pension payments needed for support provided those funds are not co-mingled with others.

(continued)

Miscellaneous:	Public assistance, workers' compensation, some crime victims' compensation, alimony and child support needed for support, medical care benefits and most life insurance proceeds.

Illinois

Homestead up to:	$7,500.
Vehicle up to:	$1,200.
Personal Property up to:	Needed clothes, health aids, school books and bibles, title certificate for a boat over twelve feet in length (vessel itself not protected), plus $2,000 of any personal property.
Tools of Trade:	$750.
Wages:	Minimum 85%.
Pension and Retirement Benefits:	Public employees' pensions and ERISA benefits.
Miscellaneous:	Workers' and unemployment compensation, social security, aid to the elderly and disabled, some personal injury and wrongful death recoveries, alimony and child support needed for support and some insurance proceeds.

Indiana

Homestead up to:	$7,500, but homestead and personal property exemption may not exceed $10,000.
Vehicle up to:	Included in personal property.
Personal Property up to:	$4,000 and health aids.
Tools of Trade:	National Guard uniforms and equipment.
Wages:	Minimum of 75%.
Pension and Retirement Benefits:	Public employees' pensions.
Miscellaneous:	Most crime victims' compensation, unemployment and workers' compensation, most life insurance policies.

Iowa

Homestead up to:	Unlimited value, but no more than 1/2 an acre in a town or forty acres elsewhere.
Vehicle up to:	$5,000 (any left over can be used to protect musical instruments and tax refunds up to $1,000).
Personal Property up to:	$1,000 of clothing, $2,000 of household goods, wedding and engagement rings, books, pictures and paintings up to $1,000, health aids, a rifle or musket and a shotgun, plus $100 of personal property.

(continued)

Tools of Trade:	Up to $10,000 of non-farming equipment, plus $10,000 of farming equipment and livestock (not including a car).
Wages:	Minimum of 90% of unpaid wages.
Pension and Retirement Benefits:	Public employees' pensions and benefits needed for support.
Miscellaneous:	Unemployment and workers' compensation, veterans' benefits, social security, AFDC, local public assistance, adopted child assistance, alimony and child support needed for support and some life insurance proceeds.

Kansas

Homestead up to:	Unlimited value, but can't be larger than one acre in a town or 160 acres elsewhere.
Vehicle up to:	$20,000 (unlimited if designed for a disabled person).
Personal Property up to:	All household goods, food, fuel and clothing to last one year, and up to $1,000 of jewelry.
Tools of Trade:	Up to $7,500, plus National Guard uniforms and equipment.
Wages:	Minimum of 75%.

(continued)

Pension and Retirement Benefits:	Public employees' pensions and ERISA benefits.
Miscellaneous:	Most public assistance benefits, workers' compensation, crime victims' compensation, certain life insurance policies and business partnership property.

Kentucky

Homestead up to:	$5,000.
Vehicle up to:	$2,500.
Personal Property up to:	$3,000 of household goods including jewelry, all health aids and $1,000 of any property.
Tools of Trade:	Farm equipment and livestock up to $3,000, non-farming tools up to $300, and a vehicle worth up to $2,500 for a mechanic, mechanical or electrical equipment servicer. Library and office equipment of professionals up to $1,000.
Wages:	Minimum of 75%.
Pension and Retirement Benefits:	State and Urban county employees', Police, Firefighter and teachers' pensions and other pensions needed for support.

(continued)

Miscellaneous:

Some personal injury and wrongful death recoveries, aid to the elderly and disabled, unemployment and workers' compensation, crime victims' compensation, alimony and child support, most insurance payments and business partnership property.

Louisiana

Homestead up to:

At least $25,000, limited to five acres in a municipality and 200 acres elsewhere.

Vehicle up to:

$0 (unprotected, but see tools of trade).

Personal Property up to:

$5,000.

Tools of Trade:

Tools, books, instruments, a vehicle and a utility trailer needed for work.

Wages:

Minimum of 75%.

Pension and Retirement Benefits:

Pensions and annuities, and ERISA qualified benefits if deposited a year before filing.

Miscellaneous:

Workers' and unemployment compensation, aid to the elderly and disabled, crime victims' compensation and certain insurance policies.

Maine

Homestead up to:	$25,000 or $50,000 if caring for dependents.
Vehicle up to:	$5,000.
Personal Property up to:	Certain kitchen appliances and supplies, health aids, jewelry up to $750, up to $200 per item of personal property, farm supplies to harvest one season's crops and up to $400 of any property. Plus up to $6,000 of unused homestead protection.
Tools of Trade:	Up to $5,000, one of each farm tool needed for raising crops and one boat not to exceed five tons for commercial fishermen.
Wages:	None.
Pension and Retirement Benefits:	Legislators', judges' and state employees' pensions, plus ERISA benefits.
Miscellaneous:	Certain wrongful death and personal injury recoveries, military equipment, unemployment and workers' compensation, veterans' benefits, social security, crime victims' compensation, AFDC, alimony and child support needed for support, some insurance policies and proceeds and business partnership property.

Maryland

Homestead up to:	$2,500 in real property.
Vehicle up to:	None.
Personal Property up to:	Clothing, household goods and pets up to $500, health aids, and any property up to $3,000.
Wages:	Minimum of 75% (varies by county).
Tools of Trade:	Up to $2,500.
Pension and Retirement Benefits:	State employees' pensions, and ERISA benefits, except IRAs.
Miscellaneous:	Unemployment and workers' compensation, crime victims' compensation, recovered lost future earnings, AFDC, most types of public assistance, some life insurance proceeds, disability and health insurance benefits, and business partnership property.

Massachusetts

Homestead up to:	Up to $300,000.
Vehicle up to:	$700.
Personal Property up to:	$3,000 of furniture, needed clothing beds and bedding, a heating unit, up to $200 of books, if no homestead exemption, up to $200 per month for rent, $75 for utilities per month, $125 in a bank account, $300 for food and some farm animals and hay.
Wages:	Up to $125 per week of earned but unpaid wages.
Tools of Trade:	Up to $500, plus up to $500 of materials you designed, plus $500 for a boat and fisherman's equipment, plus all military equipment.
Pension and Retirement Benefits:	Public employees' and Savings bank employees' pensions, private retirement benefits and ERISA qualified benefits.
Miscellaneous:	Unemployment and workers' compensation, veterans' benefits, AFDC, aid to the elderly and disabled, some disability and life insurance policies and proceeds, and business partnership property.

Michigan

Homestead up to:	$3,500, but not to exceed one lot in a town or forty acres elsewhere.
Vehicle up to:	(Included under Tools of Trade.)
Personal Property up to:	Household goods up to $1,000, up to six months of fuel, some farm animals and hay and grain.
Wages:	60% of earned but unpaid wages for the head of a household, 40% for all others.
Tools of Trade:	Up to $1,000, and all military equipment.
Pension and Retirement Benefits:	State employees' pensions, ERISA benefits and tax exempt IRAs.
Miscellaneous:	Workers' and unemployment compensation, welfare and most veterans' benefits, crime victims' compensation, most insurance policy proceeds, and business partnership property.

Minnesota

Homestead up to:	$200,000 or $500,000 if primarily used for agriculture. May not exceed 1/2 acre in a laid out or platted town or 160 acres elsewhere.
Vehicle up to:	$2,000 in 1972 constant dollars, and up to $20,000 in 1972 constant dollars for vehicle modified to serve a disabled person.
Personal Property up to:	$4,500 in 1972 constant dollars in household goods, all food, books and musical equipment.
Wages:	Minimum of 75%, though all wages can be protected for twenty days.
Tools of Trade:	Up to $5,000 in 1972 constant dollars, $7,500 in 1972 constant dollars more for farm equipment, and an unlimited amount for teaching materials.
Pension and Retirement Benefits:	State employees' pensions, ERISA qualified pensions and most IRAs needed for support.
Miscellaneous:	Workers' and unemployment compensation, crime victims' compensation, most personal injury and wrongful death recoveries, AFDC, most public benefits, veterans' benefits, most life insurance proceeds and business partnership property.

Mississippi

Homestead up to:	$75,000, but limited to 160 acres.
Vehicle up to:	(Included under personal property.)
Personal Property up to:	$10,000.
Wages:	All unpaid wages older than thirty days.
Tools of Trade:	(Included under personal property.)
Pension and Retirement Benefits:	Public employees' retirement and disability benefits, private retirement benefits, and IRAs, Keoghs, and ERISA qualified benefits deposited more than one year ago.
Miscellaneous:	Workers' and unemployment compensation, social security, aid to the disabled, crime victims' compensation, up to $10,000 in personal injury damages, most life insurance and disability insurance proceeds, and business partnership property.

Missouri

Homestead up to:	$18,000 in real property, or $1,000 in a mobile home.
Vehicle up to:	$1,000.
Personal Property up to:	Household goods up to $1,000, health aids, and jewelry up to $500. $1,250 of any property for heads of household plus $250 per child, $400 for others.
Wages:	75% of earned unpaid wages, 90% for the heads of families.
Tools of Trade:	Up to $2,000.
Pension and Retirement Benefits:	Public employees' pensions, and ERISA benefits up to $5,000.
Miscellaneous:	Workers' and unemployment compensation, social security, veterans' benefits, AFDC, alimony and child support up to $500 per month, personal injury recoveries, some life, disability and health insurance proceeds, plus business partnership property.

Montana

Homestead up to:	$100,000.
Vehicle up to:	$2,500.
Personal Property up to:	$4,500 in household goods (but no more than $600 per item), health aids, and cooperative association shares up to $500.
Wages:	75% of earned but unpaid wages.
Tools of Trade:	Up to $3,000 and all military equipment.
Pension and Retirement Benefits:	Public employees' pensions, and some ERISA benefits.
Miscellaneous:	Workers' and unemployment compensation, social security, veterans' and some welfare benefits, AFDC, aid to the elderly and disabled, crime victims' compensation, alimony and child support, and disability, illness and life insurance policy proceeds.

Nebraska

Homestead up to:	$12,500, but no more than two contiguous lots in a city or 160 acres.
Vehicle up to:	(Included under personal property.)
Personal Property up to:	$1,500 in household goods, all personal property, and $2,500 in personal property in lieu of homestead.
Wages:	85% of earned but unpaid wages for the head of a family, 75% for others.
Tools of Trade:	Up to $1,500.
Pension and Retirement Benefits:	State and county employees' pensions, military disability benefits up to $2,000, and ERISA qualified benefits needed for support.
Miscellaneous:	Workers' and unemployment compensation, AFDC, aid to the elderly and disabled, personal injury recoveries, life insurance proceeds up to $10,000, and business partnership property.

Nevada

Homestead up to:	$125,000.
Vehicle up to:	$4,500 (unlimited if equipped for the disabled).
Personal Property up to:	$3,000 in household goods, up to $1,500 of books, health aids and a gun.
Wages:	Minimum of 75% of earned but unpaid wages.
Tools of Trade:	Up to $4,500, farm equipment up to $4,500, mining equipment up to $4,500, and all military equipment.
Pension and Retirement Benefits:	Public employees' pensions.
Miscellaneous:	Unemployment compensation, industrial compensation (workers' compensation), AFDC, aid to the elderly and disabled, vocational rehabilitation benefits, most life insurance proceeds, and business partnership property.

New Hampshire

Homestead up to:	$50,000.
Vehicle up to:	$4,000.
Personal Property up to:	$3,500 in furniture, most other household goods, up to $800 of books, some farm animals and hay, jewelry up to $500, plus $1,000 of any property. Some dollar values can be shifted between categories.
Wages:	Earned but unpaid wages of the debtor and spouse.
Tools of Trade:	Up to $5,000, military equipment, and one horse or ox yoke.
Pension and Retirement Benefits:	Public employees' pensions.
Miscellaneous:	Workers' and unemployment compensation, AFDC, aid to the elderly and disabled, child support, most life insurance proceeds, and business partnership property.

New Jersey

Homestead up to:	None.
Vehicle up to:	(Included under personal property.)
Personal Property up to:	$1,000, plus $1,000 of household goods.
Wages:	Minimum of 90%, all military wages.

(continued)

Tools of Trade:	None.
Pension and Retirement Benefits:	Most government employees' pensions, and ERISA qualified benefits.
Miscellaneous:	Workers' and unemployment compensation, most old age and disability assistance, crime victims' compensation in escrow, most life insurance proceeds, health and disability insurance benefits, and military disability and death benefits.

New Mexico

Homestead up to:	$30,000 if married, widowed, or supporting another.
Vehicle up to:	$4,000.
Personal Property up to:	All household goods, $2,500 of jewelry, $500 of any property, plus up to $2,000 of any property in lieu of the homestead exemption, building materials, and enough shares in a cooperative to remain a member.
Wages:	Minimum of 75% of earned but unpaid wages.
Tools of Trade:	Up to $1,500, plus all equipment needed to operate or repair an oil line, gas well or pipeline.

(continued)

Pension and Retirement Benefits:	Any pension or retirement benefits.
Miscellaneous:	Unemployment and workers' compensation, AFDC, most welfare, life insurance proceeds, ownership in an unincorporated association, and business partnership property.

New York

Homestead up to:	Normally $10,000.
Vehicle up to:	$2,400.
Personal Property up to:	Most household goods, books up to $50, a $35 watch and domestic animals and food worth up to $450. Plus up to $2,500 cash in lieu of homestead.
Wages:	90% of earned but unpaid wages received with in sixty days of filing.
Tools of Trade:	Up to $600, plus military equipment.
Pension and Retirement Benefits:	Public retirement benefits, ERISA qualified plans, Keoghs, and IRAs needed for support.

(continued)

Miscellaneous:	Unemployment benefits, veterans' benefits, social security, AFDC, aid to the elderly and disabled, crime victims' compensation, some welfare, alimony and child support needed for support, most life disability and illness insurance proceeds and business partnership property.

North Carolina

Homestead up to:	Up to $10,000, first $3,500 of unused homestead exemption can be used to portect other property.
Vehicle up to:	$1,500.
Personal Property up to:	$3,500, plus $750 per dependent (up to four).
Wages:	Earned but unpaid wages earned within sixty days of filing bankruptcy.
Tools of Trade:	Up to $750.
Pension and Retirement Benefits:	Most state, county and municipal employees' pensions and individual retirement plans.
Miscellaneous:	Unemployment and workers' compensation, crime victims' compensation, personal injury and wrongful death recoveries, certain types of government aid, most life insurance policies and proceeds, and business partnership property.

North Dakota

Homestead up to:	$80,000.
Vehicle up to:	$1,200.
Personal Property:	*Anyone* may claim clothing, one year of fuel, books up to $100, crops and grains raised on the debtor's land, and pictures. Up to $7,500 of unused homestead, and up to $2,500 of any property if crops are not claimed.

The *Head of a Household* not claiming crops may claim $5,000 of any property OR up to $1,000 of furniture, $1,500 of books and musical instruments, professional tools and/or library up to $1,000, tools of a mechanic and/or stock in trade up to $1,000, and farm implements and livestock up to $4,500.

PLUS clothing, one year of fuel, books up to $100 and pictures.

ALL OTHERS: $2,500 of any personal property.

Wages:	Minimum of 75% of earned but unpaid wages or forty times the minimum wage.
Tools of Trade:	(Included under personal property.)

(continued)

Pension and Retirement Benefits:	Public employees' and disabled veterans' pensions, plus most private retirement benefits.
Miscellaneous:	Unemployment and workers' compensation, social security, crime victims' compensation, life insurance proceeds and most life insurance policies.

Ohio

Homestead up to:	$5,000.
Vehicle up to:	$1,000.
Personal Property up to:	Household goods, jewelry, books, animals, musical instruments, firearms and crops up to $200 per item, plus one piece of jewelry up to $400, total may not exceed $2,000 or $1,500 if homestead is claimed. Plus clothing, beds and bedding up to $200 per item, cooking unit and refrigerator up to $300 each, cash and cash due up to $400, health aids, and up to $400 of any property.
Wages:	Minimum of 75% of earned but unpaid wages.
Tools of Trade:	Up to $750.
Pension and Retirement Benefits:	Public employees' pensions, IRAs, Keoghs and ERISA qualified benefits.

(continued)

Miscellaneous:	Workers' and unemployment compensation, disability assistance, crime victims' compensation, wrongful death recoveries, personal injury recoveries not including pain and suffering up to $5,000, compensation for future lost earnings needed for support, alimony and child support needed for support, most life insurance proceeds, disability benefits up to $600 per month and business partnership property.

Oklahoma

Homestead up to:	Unlimited if not over 1/4 acre, otherwise up to $5,000 on one acre in a city or 160 acres elsewhere.
Vehicle up to:	$3,000.
Personal Property up to:	$4,000 of clothing, all furniture, books, portraits, pictures, a gun and health aids, one year of food, two bridles and two saddles, 100 chickens, twenty sheep, ten hogs, five cows, two horses and forage for livestock to last one year.
Wages:	75% of wages earned ninety days before filing bankruptcy.
Tools of Trade:	Up to $5,000.

(continued)

Pension and Retirement Benefits:	Firefighters', police officers', county employees', disabled veterans' law enforcement employees' and teachers' pensions, ERISA qualified pensions, and tax exempt benefits.
Miscellaneous:	Unemployment compensation, social security, crime victims' compensation, AFDC, and personal injury, workers' compensation and wrongful death recoveries up to $50,000, alimony and child support, life insurance policies and proceeds, and business partnership property.

Oregon

Homestead up to:	$25,000 on land you own (up to $33,000 if jointly owned), or $23,000 for a mobile home on land you don't own (up to $30,000 if jointly owned).
Vehicle up to:	$1,700.

(continued)

Personal Property up to:	$1,800 of clothing, jewelry and personal items, $3,000 of household items, all health aids, books, pictures and musical instruments up to $600, sixty days of food and fuel, domestic animals and poultry plus sixty days feed worth up to $1,000, and $400 of personal property (though this can not be used to increase the cap on an existing exemption.)
Wages:	Minimum of 75% of earned but unpaid wages.
Tools of Trade:	Up to $3,000.
Pension and Retirement Benefits:	Government employees' pensions and ERISA-qualified benefits.
Miscellaneous:	Workers' and unemployment compensation, crime victims' compensation, most forms of government and medical assistance, alimony and child support needed for support, most life insurance proceeds and business partnership property.

Pennsylvania

Homestead up to:	None.
Vehicle up to:	(Included under personal property.)
Personal Property up to:	$300 of any property, plus clothing, Bibles, school books and uniforms and accoutrements.
Wages:	Earned but unpaid wages.
Tools of Trade:	None.
Pension and Retirement Benefits:	Municipal, county and state employees' retirement benefits, self-employment benefits, and some private retirement benefits.
Miscellaneous:	Workers' and unemployment compensation, veterans' benefits, most insurance benefits, and business partnership property.

Rhode Island

Homestead up to:	$150,000.
Vehicle up to:	(Included under personal property.)
Personal Property up to:	$8,600, plus clothing, up to $300 of books, debt owed to you on a promissory note, and one corpse.
Wages:	Earned but unpaid wages, usually up to $50.

(continued)

Tools of Trade:	Up to $1,200 and a practicing professional's library.
Pension and Retirement Benefits:	State, municipal and private employees' pensions, and ERISA-qualified pensions.
Miscellaneous:	Workers' and unemployment compensation, most government aid, most insurance proceeds and business partnership property.

South Carolina

Homestead up to:	$5,000.
Vehicle up to:	$1,200.
Personal Property up to:	$2,500, $500 of jewelry, plus $1,000 if no homestead is claimed.
Wages:	None.
Tools of Trade:	Up to $750.
Pension and Retirement Benefits:	Public employees' pensions and ERISA-qualified pensions.
Miscellaneous:	Unemployment and workers' compensation, most government aid, alimony and child support, personal injury and wrongful death recoveries most insurance proceeds and business partnership property.

South Dakota

Homestead up to:	Unlimited value if not over one acre in a town or 160 acres elsewhere. Mobile homes can also be protected up to an unlimited value if not larger than 240 square feet and if have been in South Dakota for at least 6 months before the bankruptcy is filed.
Vehicle up to:	(Included under personal property.)
Personal Property up to:	$2,000 if not the head of a family. If the head of a family, personal property up to $4,000 OR furniture up to $200, books and musical instruments up to $200, tools and library of a professional up to $300, tools of a mechanic up to $200, farm equipment up to $1,250, two yoke of oxen or span of horses, two cows, five swine, twenty-five sheep and one year of food.
Wages:	Earned wages owed sixty days prior to filing needed for support.
Tools of Trade:	(Included under personal property.)
Pension and Retirement Benefits:	Public employees' pensions.
Miscellaneous:	Unemployment and workers' compensation, AFDC, most life insurance proceeds and health benefits and business partnership property.

Tennessee

Homestead up to:	$5,000 or $7,500 for joint owners.
Vehicle up to:	(Included under personal property.)
Personal Property up to:	$4,000 plus clothing, storage containers, school books, pictures, portraits and a Bible.
Wages:	Minimum of 75% of earned but unpaid wages.
Tools of Trade:	Up to $1,000.
Pension and Retirement Benefits:	Public employees' and teachers' pensions and ERISA benefits.
Miscellaneous:	Unemployment and workers' compensation, most government benefits, alimony owed at least thirty days prior to filing bankruptcy, lost earnings, most personal injury recoveries up to $7,500, wrongful death recoveries up to $10,000, disability and illness benefits and some life insurance proceeds.

Texas

Homestead up to:	Unlimited, but can not exceed ten acres in a town or 100 acres elsewhere (200 acres for a family).
Vehicle up to:	One motor vehicle (but see personal property).
Personal Property up to:	All home furnishings, food, clothing, up to $7,500 of jewelry, two firearms, sports equipment, two horses or mules with riding equipment, twelve cattle, sixty other livestock, 120 fowl, feed for these animals and household pets. LIMIT: vehicles, personal property, owed wages and tools of trade cannot exceed $30,000 (or $60,000 for the head of a household).
Wages:	Current wages for personal services, but may not exceed $7,500 (also see personal property).
Tools of Trade:	Tools, books and equipment, including motor vehicles, boats, farming and ranch vehicles and instruments used in a trade or profession.
Pension and Retirement Benefits:	State employees', law enforcement officers' survivors', police officers', firefighters' and municipal employees' pensions, church benefits and ERISA qualified benefits.

(continued)

Miscellaneous:

Unemployment and workers' compensation, AFDC, crime victims' compensation, medical assistance, most insurance proceeds, and business partnership property.

Utah

Homestead up to:

$20,000 if primary residence or up to $5,000 otherwise.

Vehicle up to:

(Included under tools of trade.)

Personal Property up to:

All clothing except jewelry and furs, refrigerator, freezer, stove, washer, dryer, sewing machine, needed health aids, twelve months of food, beds and bedding, furnishings and appliances up to $500, books, instruments and animals up to $500, heirlooms and sentimental items up to $500.

Wages:

Minimum of 75% of earned but unpaid wages.

Tools of Trade:

Military property of a national guard member, a motor vehicle used in a business or trade up to $2,500, and tools books and implements up to $3,500.

(continued)

Pension and Retirement Benefits:	Public employees' pensions, ERISA-qualified pensions and any pension needed for support.
Miscellaneous:	Workers' compensation, crime victims' compensation, veterans' benefits, personal injury and wrongful death recoveries, child support, alimony needed for support, medical benefits, life insurance policies up to $5,000 or needed for support, and business partnership property.

Vermont

Homestead up to:	$75,000.
Vehicle up to:	$2,500.
Personal Property up to:	$2,500 of clothing, goods, furnishings, appliances, books, musical instruments, animals and crops, one of each major household appliance, health aids, $700 of bank deposits, $500 of jewelry plus a wedding ring, 500 gallons of oil, five tons of coal or ten cords of firewood, 500 gallons of bottled gas, one cow, ten sheep, ten chickens, three swarms of bees and feed to last one winter, one yoke of oxen or steer, two horses, two harnesses, two halters, two chains, one plow, and crops growing up to $5,000.

(continued)

Wages:	Minimum of 85% of earned but unpaid wages.
Tools of Trade:	Up to $5,000.
Pension and Retirement Benefits:	State employees' teachers' and municipal employees' pensions, and self-directed accounts, including IRAs and Keoghs up to certain dollar amounts.
Miscellaneous:	Workers' and unemployment compensation, plus veterans' benefits, social security, alimony, child support and crime victims' compensation needed for support, lost future earnings, personal injury and wrongful death recoveries, some life insurance policies, health benefits, and business partnership property.

Virginia

Homestead up to:	$5,000 ($7,000 for some veterans) plus $500 per dependent.
Vehicle up to:	$2,000 if you are a householder.

(continued)

Personal Property up to:	Any unused homestead and if you are a householder: clothing up to $1,000, household furnishings up to $5,000, family portraits and heirlooms up to $5,000, wedding and engagement rings, family Bible, pets and prescribed health aids, plus $2,000 of any property if you are a disabled veteran.
Wages:	Minimum of 75% or earned but unpaid wages.
Tools of Trade:	Military equipment, and a householder may claim: tools, books, instruments, machines (including motor vehicles), vessels and aircraft up to $10,000, plus a farmer householder may claim a tractor, wagon, cart, horses, a pair of mules with gear up to $3,000, fertilizer, two plows, harvest cradle, two iron wages, pitchfork and rake up to $1,000.
Pension and Retirement Benefits:	State pensions.
Miscellaneous:	Unemployment and workers' compensation, aid to the aged and disabled, crime victims' compensation, most life insurance proceeds, health benefits and business partnership property.

Washington

Homestead up to:	$40,000.
Vehicle up to:	Two motor vehicles up to $2,500.
Personal Property up to:	Clothing (not furs), jewelry and furs up to $1,000, household goods up to $2,700, books and private libraries up to $2,500, all keepsakes and pictures, plus $1,000 of any property (but no more than $100 in cash, stocks or bonds).
Wages:	Minimum of 75% of earned but unpaid wages.
Tools of Trade:	Up to $5,000.
Pension and Retirement Benefits:	Public employees' pensions, volunteer firefighter pensions, and ERISA-qualified benefits.
Miscellaneous:	Unemployment and workers' compensation, crime victims' compensation, most health and old age assistance, most life insurance proceeds, and business partnership property.

West Virginia

Homestead up to:	$15,000.
Vehicle up to:	$2,400.
Personal Property up to:	Clothing, household goods, furnishings, appliances, books, musical instruments, animals and crops up to $8,000, but no more than $400 per item. Any unused portion of the homestead exemption.
Wages:	80% of earned but unpaid wages.
Tools of Trade:	Up to $1,500.
Pension and Retirement Benefits:	Public employees' and teachers' pensions, and ERISA-qualified benefits needed for support.
Miscellaneous:	Workers' and unemployment compensation, veterans' benefits, social security, and aid to the aged and disabled, alimony and child support needed for support, most life insurances policies and proceeds, and business partnership property.

Wisconsin

Homestead up to:	$40,000.
Vehicle up to:	$1,200 (plus any unused household exemption).
Personal Property up to:	Household goods, including jewelry, sporting goods and animals up to $5,000.
Wages:	75% of net wages, but limited to the amount needed for support.
Tools of Trade:	Up to $7,500.
Pension and Retirement Benefits:	Public employees' pension and private retirement benefits.
Miscellaneous:	Unemployment and workers' compensation, crime victims' compensation, veterans' benefits, AFDC and other social services payments, wrongful death and lost wage recoveries, alimony and child support needed for support, most life insurance proceeds and policies and business partnership property.

Wyoming

Homestead up to:	$10,000 of real property or a trailer up to $6,000.
Vehicle up to:	$2,400.
Personal Property up to:	$1,000 of clothing and a wedding ring, household items up to $2,000, school books pictures and a Bible.
Wages:	Minimum of 75% of earned but unpaid wages, and earnings of a national guard member.
Tools of Trade:	Up to $2,000 (can include a motor vehicle).
Pension and Retirement Benefits:	Public and private retirement benefits.
Miscellaneous:	Unemployment and workers' compensation, crime victims' compensation, AFDC and other government assistance, most life insurance policies, and some disability benefits.

Index

About the Authors

Wendell Schollander received his BA in Economics and his MBA from the Wharton School of Finance at the University of Pennsylvania. He received his law degree from Duke University. Mr. Schollander has practiced law in the corporate and bankruptcy fields for more than thirty years. He served as general counsel of RJR Archer and the Specialty Tobacco Counsel. Mr. Schollander currently practices law in Winston-Salem, North Carolina.

Wes Schollander received his BA from the University of North Carolina and his JD from Wake Forest School of Law. He is a member of the North Carolina Bar Association and the North Carolina Young Lawyers Association. Mr. Schollander practices law in Winston-Salem, North Carolina.